New-Age and Traditional Tools to Ease the Job Search Pain Including CareerBuilder, LinkedIn, and Employment Agencies

Lyle Simon

The role of the book within our culture is changing. The change is brought on by new ways to acquire & use content, the rapid dissemination of information and real-time peer collaboration on a global scale. Despite these changes one thing is clear--"the book" in it's traditional form continues to play an important role in learning and communication. The book you are holding in your hands utilizes the unique characteristics of the Internet -- relying on web infrastructure and collaborative tools to share and use resources in keeping with the characteristics of the medium (user-created, defying control, etc.)--while maintaining all the convenience and utility of a real book.

Contents

Articles

Prepare for Job Interviews

Unemployment Benefits

References

Job Hunting via Employment Websites

Job hunting

Job hunting, **job seeking**, or **job searching** is the act of looking for employment, due to unemployment or discontent with a current position. The immediate goal of job seeking is usually to obtain a job interview with an employer which may lead to getting hired. The job hunter or seeker typically first looks for job vacancies or employment opportunities.

Steps

Locating jobs

Common methods of job hunting are:

- Finding a job through a friend or an extended business network, personal network, or online social network service
- Using a job search engine
- Looking through the classifieds in newspapers
- Using a private or public employment agency or recruiter
- Looking on a company's web site for open jobs, typically in its applicant tracking system
- Going to a job fair

As of 2010, less than 10% of U.S. jobs are filled through online ads.

Researching the employers

Many job seekers research the employers to which they are applying, and some employers see evidence of this as a positive sign of enthusiasm for the position or the company, or as a mark of thoroughness. Information collected might include open positions, full name, locations, web site, business description, year established, revenues, number of employees, stock price if public, name of chief executive officer, major products or services, major competitors, and strengths and weaknesses.

Networking

Contacting as many people as possible is a highly effective way to find a job. It is estimated that 60% or higher of all jobs are found through networking. Job recruiters may use online social networking sites for this purpose.[citation needed]

Applying

One can also go and hand out résumés or Curriculum Vitae to prospective employers. Another recommended method of job hunting is cold calling or emailing companies that one desires to work for and inquire to whether there are any job vacancies.

After finding a desirable job, they would then apply for the job by responding to the advertisement. This may mean applying through a website, emailing or mailing in a hard copy of your résumé to a prospective employer. It is generally recommended that résumés be brief, organized, concise, and targeted to the position being sought. With certain occupations, such as graphic design or writing, portfolios of a job seeker's previous work are essential and are evaluated as much, if not more than the person's résumé. In most other occupations, the résumé should focus on past accomplishments, expressed in terms as concretely as possible (e.g. number of people managed, amount of increased sales or improved customer satisfaction).

Interviewing

Main article: job interview

Once an employer has received your résumé, they will make a list of potential employees to be interviewed based on the résumé and any other information contributed. During the interview process, interviewers generally look for persons who they believe will be best for the job and work environment. The interview may occur in several rounds until the interviewer is satisfied and offers the job to the applicant.

Onboarding

Main article: onboarding

New employees begin their onboarding into new organizations even before their first contact with potential employers. While the best employers will invest in accommodating, assimilating and accelerating new employees, those joining firms that don't should take charge of their own onboarding, doing their best to get a head start before their start, manage their messages, and help others deliver results after they start.

Job hunting in economic theory

Economists use the term 'frictional unemployment' to mean unemployment resulting from the time and effort that must be expended before an appropriate job is found. Search theory is the economic theory that studies the optimal decision of how much time and effort to spend searching, and which offers to accept or reject (in the context of a job hunt, or likewise in other contexts like searching for a low price).

See also

- Employment counsellor
- Job-seeking expense tax deductions
- Precarious work
- Search theory

External links

- State Employment Offices (U.S.) [1]

Employment website

An **employment website** is a web site dealing specifically with employment or careers. Many employment websites are designed to allow employers to post job requirements for a position to be filled and are commonly known as job boards. Other employment sites offer employer reviews, career and job-search advice describe different job descriptions or employers. Through a job website a prospective employee can locate and fill out a job application or submit resumes over the Internet for the advertised position.

History

The Online Career Center launched in 1993 as a non-profit organization backed by forty major corporations as a system for job hunters to store their resumes within the databases as well as for recruiters to post job openings to the databases.

In 1994 Robert J. McGovern began NetStart Inc. as software sold to companies for listing job openings on their Web sites and manage the incoming e-mails those listings generated. After an influx of two million dollars in investment capital he then transported this software to its own web address, at first listing the job openings from the companies who utilized the software. NetStart Inc. changed its name in 1998 to operate under the name of their software, CareerBuilder. The company received a further influx of seven million dollars from investment firms such as New Enterprise Associates to expand their operations.

Six major newspapers joined forces in 1995 to list their classified sections online. The service was called CareerPath.com and featured help-wanted listings from the Los Angeles Times, the Boston Globe, Chicago Tribune, the New York Times, San Jose Mercury News and the Washington Post.

The industry attempted to reach a broader, less tech-savvy base in 1998 when Hotjobs.com attempted to buy a Super Bowl spot, but Fox rejected the ad for being in poor taste. The ad featured a janitor at a zoo sweeping out the Elephant cage completely unbeknownst to the animal. The elephant sits down briefly and when it stands back up, the janitor has disappeared. The ad meant to illustrate a need for those stuck in jobs they hate, and offer a solution through their Web site. Hotjobs.com promplty fired the advertising agency who created the ad.

Monster.com gambled on a 1999 Super Bowl ad. CEO Jeff Taylor authorized three 30 second spots for a total of four million dollars. The ad which featured children speaking like adults, drolly intoning their dream of working at various dead-end jobs to humorous effect were far more popular than rival Hotjobs.com ad about a security guard who transitions from a low paying security job to the same job at a fancier building.Monster.com was elevated to the top spot of online employment sites. Hotjobs.com's ad wasn't as successful, but it gave the company enough of a boost for its IPO in August.

After being purchased in a joint venture by Knight Ridder and Tribune Company in July, CareerBuilder absorbed competitor boards CareerPath.com and then Headhunter.net which had already acquired CareerMosaic. Even with these aggressive mergers CareerBuilder still trailed behind the number one employment site Jobsonline.com, number two Monster.com and number three Hotjobs.com.

Monster.com made a move in 2001 to purchase Hotjobs.com for $374 million in stock, but were unsuccessful due to Yahoo's unsolicited cash and stock bid of $430 million late in the year. Yahoo had previously announced plans to enter the job board business, but decided to jump start that venture by purchasing the established brand. By August 2002, Monster.com posted a loss of $504 million forcing COO James Treacy to resign.

Features and types

Job postings

A **job board** is a website that facilitates job hunting and range from large scale generalist sites to niche job boards for job categories such as engineering, legal, insurance, social work, teaching as well as cross-sector categories such as green jobs, ethical jobs and seasonal jobs. Users can typically deposit their résumés and submit them to potential employers, while employers can post job ads and search for potential employees.

The term **job search engine** might refer to a job board with a search engine style interface, or to a web site that actually indexes and searches other web sites.

As of July 2009 and according to comScore Media Metrix, the most visited job boards were CareerBuilder, Yahoo! HotJobs, and Monster.com.

Metasearch and vertical search engines

Some web sites are simply search engines that collect results from multiple independent job boards. This is an example of both metasearch (since these are search engines which search other search engines) and vertical search (since the searches are limited to a specific topic - job listings).

Some of these new search engines primarily index traditional job boards. These sites aim to provide a "one-stop shop" for job-seekers who don't need to search the underlying job boards. In 2006, tensions developed between the job boards and several scraper sites, with Craigslist banning scrapers from its job classifieds and Monster.com specifically banning scrapers through its adoption of a robots exclusion standard on all its pages while others have embraced them.

Other job search engines index pages only from employers' websites, such as LinkUp, Indeed, Hound, and Eluta.ca (Canada) choosing to bypass traditional job boards entirely. These vertical search engines allow jobseekers to find new positions that may not be advertised on the traditional job boards.

Employer review website

An **employer review website** is a type of employment website where past and current employees post comments about their experiences working for a company or organization. An employer review website normally takes the form of an internet forum. Typical comments are about management, working conditions, and pay. Although employer review websites may produce links to potential employers, they do not typically list vacancies.[citation needed]

Pay For Performance (PFP)

The most recent second generation of employment websites, often referred to as **Pay For Performance** (PFP) involves charging for membership services rendered to jobseekers. The PFP category is expected to expand as consumers become more sophisticated and the universe of employment sites has become more cluttered.

Industry structure

The success of jobs search engines in bridging the gap between jobseekers and employers has spawned thousands of job sites, many of which list job opportunities in a specific sector, such as education, health care, hospital management, academics and even in the non-governmental sector. These sites range from broad all-purpose job boards, to niche sites that serve various audiences, geographies, and industries. Many industry experts are encouraging jobseekers to concentrate on industry specific sector sites. With the increase in popularity of niche sites, other sites have begun to rank them in order of quality.

Venture capital, mergers and acquisitions have been active in the job board industry for more than a decade. In 2008, several private equity firms started the process of piecing together large job board networks while other firms attempted to expand through acquisition.

Risks

Many jobs search engines and jobs boards encourage users to post their resume and contact details. While this is attractive for the site operators (who sell access to the resume bank to headhunters and recruiters), job-seekers exercise caution in uploading personal information, since they have no control over where their resume will eventually be seen. Their resume may be viewed by a current employer or, worse, by fraudsters who may use information from it to amass and sell personal contact information, or even perpetrate identity theft.

See also

* Job wrapping

Job wrapping

Job wrapping is a term used commonly to describe a process by which jobs can be captured from employer website and posted to the job boards that the employer wants to advertise them.

Corporate recruiters and HR professionals who send job listings to multiple Internet employment sites can sometimes delegate those chores to the employment sites themselves under an arrangement called "job wrapping". Job wrap ensures that employer job openings and updates get wrapped up regularly and posted on the job boards that they have designated.

The term "job wrapping" is synonymous with "spidering", "scraping", or "mirroring".

Job wrapping is generally done by a third party vendor .

CareerBuilder

URL	www.careerbuilder.com [1]
Commercial?	Yes
Type of site	Job Search Engine
Registration	Optional
Available language(s)	English, Hindi, German, Swedish, French, Spanish, Greek, Romanian, Dutch, Italian
Owner	Gannett Co, Inc. (50.8%) Tribune Company (30.8%) The McClatchy Company (14.4%) Microsoft Corp. (4%)
Created by	Rob McGovern
Launched	1995
Alexa rank	424
Revenue	▲$542 Million USD (2009)
Current status	Active

CareerBuilder.com is the largest online employment website in the United States, with more than 23 million unique visitors each month and a 34% market share of help-wanted web sites in the United States. CareerBuilder.com provides online career search services for more than 1,900 partners as of March 2008, including 140 newspapers and portals such as AOL and MSN. It was founded in 1994.

Careerbuilder.com is jointly owned by the Gannett Company, The McClatchy Company and the Tribune Company. A 2007 deal was completed, in which Microsoft will acquire a minority stake in the firm and continue its relationship through 2013 with CareerBuilder as the exclusive content provider for the MSN Careers channel.

On September 3, 2008, Gannett acquired an additional 10% stake in CareerBuilder from Tribune for $135 million. Ownership stakes as of that date are as follows: Gannett (50.8%), Tribune (30.8%), McClatchy (14.4%), and Microsoft (4%).

Company Information

CareerBuilder.com is headquartered in Chicago, Illinois, has more than 2,500 employees, and is under the leadership of CEO Matt Ferguson. It was founded in 1994 by Rob McGovern, who is now the CEO/founder of Jobfox.

After several years of profit, CareerBuilder.com suffered challenges related to the economic downturn in 2008. The company announced layoffs in December 2008, affecting approximately 300 employees. [2]

History

Career Builder began in 1994 as NetStart Inc. selling software to companies for listing job openings on their Web sites and the ability to manage the incoming e-mails those listings created. After an influx of two million dollars in investment capital the company transported this software, named CareerBuilder to its own web address, at first listing the job openings from the companies who utilized the software. NetStart Inc. changed its name in 1998 to operate under the name of their software, CareerBuilder. The newly christened company received a further influx of seven million dollars from investment firms such as New Enterprise Associates to expand their operations.

The company announced their decision to go public in April 1999. The company's IPO on May 12, 1999 raised $8 million more than initially forecast, but was less successful than other Net offerings of the time. In its first day of trading, the stock opened at $17.50 and rose as high as $20 before closing at $16. Microsoft moved quickly to acquire a minority stake in the company in exchange for using the company's database on their own web portal.

After being purchased in a joint venture by Knight Ridder and Tribune Company in July 2000 for $8 a share CareerBuilder absorbed competitor boards CareerPath.com and then Headhunter.net which had already acquired CareerMosaic. Even with these aggressive mergers CareerBuilder still trailed behind the number one employment site Jobsonline.com, number two Monster.com and number three Hotjobs.com.

In 2001, major newspapers owned by Knight Ridder and the Tribune Company merged their help wanted sections with the online component. Rob McGovern was replaced as CEO in March 2002 by Robert Montgomery. Gannett purchased a one-third interest in the company for $98.3 million in 2002, adding the CareerBuilder brand to its 90 newspapers nationwide.

The McClatchy Company purchased Knight Ridder $4.5 billion in stock and cash in March 2006.

Awards

In April 2006 CareerBuilder.com's site was nominated for a Webby Award in the employment category.

In December 2007, CareerBuilder.com won the Stevie Award for excellence in Customer Service.

In June 2008 CareerBuilder.com won the International Customer Management Institute's Global Call Center of the Year Award.

Partnerships

- South Korea - Incruit

Consumer complaints

According to two consumer complaints received by the office of Illinois Attorney General, Lisa Madigan, and reports from other states, scam artists have been contacting job hunters through CareerBuilder.com regarding a "Donations Handler" position with an international charity. The agreement is a classic pigeon drop. The "handler" accepts checks sent in the mail from Atlanta, Georgia and is required to wire transfer the amount to an international account within 24 hours. The checks are later discovered to be fraudulent. Victims reported losing between $500 and $2,000 in this scheme.

See also

- Monster.com
- Hotjobs
- Fins.com

External links

- www.careerbuilder.com [1]
- Work for CareerBuilder [3]
- Salary Calculator by CareerBuilder.com [4]

Incruit

For the search engine produced by Incruit Corporation., see the article on Incruit.

Type	Public (KOSDAQ: 060300 [1])
Founded	Seocho-gu, Seoul, Korea (1998)
Headquarters	Gangnam-gu, Seoul, Korea
Key people	Kwangsug Lee, Co-founder/CEO/Chairman of the board Miyoung Seo, Co-founder/Vice President of Incruit
Products	List of Incruit services and tools
Employees	250 est. (2007)
Website	http://www.incruit.com [2]

Incruit Corporation (Hangul:인크루트, KRX: 060300 [3]), is an Internet corporation, established in 1998, that manages the Incruit.com providing Internet Resume and jobs. Incruit Corporation is headquartered at the Seoul in Korea, and employs over 200 people. Incruit is the first Internet recruiting marketplace site between job seekers and companies and has the first Internet Résumé made of database (June 1. 1998). And it operates an HR media portal for the companies who want to hire employees and for the jobseekers who want new job opportunities.

Incruit Portal is recognized as HR marketing platform by companies to be a preferred employer.[citation needed] Incruit is first made in 1998 by Kwangsug Lee and Miyoung Seo.

Partnerships

* United States - CareerBuilder

Competitors

* Zeniel
* 21 Agency Company

External links

* http://www.incruit.com/(Korea)
* http://in.incruit.com/(India)
* Incruit English Homepage [4]

Monster.com

URL	http://www.monster.com/
Slogan	"Your calling is calling"
Commercial?	Yes
Type of site	Job search engine
Registration	Optional
Available language(s)	Multilingual
Owner	Monster Worldwide
Created by	Monster Worldwide, Inc.
Launched	1999
Alexa rank	483
Revenue	Banner ads, referral marketing
Current status	Active

Monster.com is one of the largest employment websites in the world, owned and operated by Monster Worldwide, Inc. Monster is one of the 20 most visited websites out of 100 million worldwide, according to comScore Media Metrics (November 2006). It was created in 1999 by the merger of The Monster Board (TMB) and Online Career Center (OCC), which were two of the first and most popular career web sites on the Internet. Monster is primarily used to help those seeking work to find job openings that match their skills and location.

Today, Monster is the largest job search engine in the world, with over a million job postings at any time and over 150 million resumes in the database (2008) and over 63 million job seekers per month. The company employs approximately 5,000 employees in 36 countries. Its headquarters are in Maynard, Massachusetts.

Monster also maintains the Monster Employment Index.

Jeff Taylor founded The Monster Board and served as CEO and "Chief Monster" for many years.

History

Jeff Taylor contracted Christopher Caldwell of Net Daemons Associates to develop a facility in an NDA lab on a Sun Microsystems Sparc 5 where job seekers could search a job database with a web browser. The machine was moved to sit under a router in a phone closet in Adion (a human resources company owned by Taylor) when the site went live in April 1994.

Initially, the site was populated with job descriptions from the newspaper segment of Adion's business with the permissions of the companies advertising the jobs.

Later in 1994, The Monster Board issued a press release that was picked up and provided needed exposure to drive people to the web site. Monster was the first public job search on the Internet; first public resume database in the world and the first to have job search agents or job alerts.

When TMP acquired Adion, the site was moved into BBN Planet's web hosting facility where it grew from 3 SPARC-1000s to become the centerpiece of the globally distributed network it is today.

TMP went public in December 1996, with its shares traded on Nasdaq under the symbol "TMPW". In 1998, TMP acquisitions expanded the Recruitment Advertising network. TMP became one of the largest recruitment advertising agencies in the world.

In June 1998, The Monster Board moved its corporate headquarters out of a small office above a Chinese restaurant in downtown Framingham, Massachusetts to an old textile mill in Maynard, Massachusetts that formerly housed Digital Equipment Corporation.

In January 1999, The Monster Board became known as Monster.com after merging with Online Career Center, another of TMP Worldwide's properties. The first post-merger president of the new Monster.com business was Bill Warren, the founder of Online Career Center. Bill Warren received the 1997 Employment Management Association's prestigious Pericles Pro Meritus Award, an honor presented by EMA/SHRM in recognition of being the founder of online recruiting on the Internet.

In November 2000, seeking to capture the entry-level job market, Monster acquired JOBTRAK, which at the time had partnerships with more than 1,500 college and university career centers. JOBTRAK was founded in 1987 by Connie Ramberg, Ken Ramberg and David Franey. Monster rebranded JOBTRAK as MonsterTRAK and continues to operate the site to target college students and alumni seeking jobs and career advice.

Recognizing that job hunting often leads to relocation, Monster launched Monstermoving.com in 2000 to provide consumers with the comprehensive resources necessary for a successful move.

TMP Worldwide was added to S&P 500 Index in 2001. TMP Worldwide changed its corporate name to Monster Worldwide, Inc. and began trading under the new Nasdaq ticker symbol "MNST" in 2003.

Monster.com advertised on the Super Bowl starting in 1999 and every year through Super Bowl XXXVIII. Monster's first-ever Super Bowl ad, "When I Grow Up," (created by Mullen) asking job seekers, "What did you want to be?" It is the only commercial named to *Time* magazine's list of the "Best Television of 1999." As the official online career management services sponsor of the 2002

Olympic Winter Games and 2002 U.S. Olympic Team, Monster had a strong presence at the 2002 Olympic Winter Games in Salt Lake City.

In April 2002 Monster purchased the Jobs.com URL and Trademark for $800,000. Then Founder and Chairman Jeff Taylor was quoted as saying "Jobs.com is a desirable URL."

In August 2005, founder Jeff Taylor left Monster to create Eons.com.

In April 2007, Monster named Sal Iannuzzi as chairman and CEO.

In May 2007 Monster launched their first (NA and EU) Mobile services offering Mobile job search and career advice [1].

In July 2008 Monster acquired Trovix, a semantic job search engine, for USD $72.5 million. Monster has indicated that it plans to replace their job search and candidate matching with Trovix's technology.

In February 2010, it was announced that Monster would acquire its rival, HotJobs, from Yahoo! for $225 million dollars. Monster also established a traffic sharing agreement with Yahoo! as part of the deal, seeing it become Yahoo's official job site for 3 years.

Criticism

Monster has recently been to blame in several instances of personal information theft. In less than two weeks, in August 2007, Monster had numerous leaks that resulted in the loss of millions of customers' data to identity theft. Although Monster waited several days to announce this leak (drawing heavy criticism), they subsequently announced new security measures to prevent this happening again.

However, in January 2009, there was another large scale leak at its UK based site monster.co.uk, in which demographic information of up to 4.5 million people was obtained by hackers.

Stock option grants backdating scandal

Backdating an option means retroactively setting the option's strike price to a day when the stock traded at a different price. A call (buy) option with a lower strike price is more valuable because it's less expensive to exercise, while the inverse is true for a put (sell) option. The practice is not necessarily illegal, but must be disclosed to shareholders. In July 2006, the company said it might restate financial results for the year that ended December 31, 2005, and previous years to record additional noncash charges for stock-based compensation expenses relating to various stock option grants.

In September 2006, Monster suspended Myron Olesnyckyj pending the internal review irregular stock option grants. He had held the titles of senior vice president, general counsel and secretary.

On October 9, 2006 Monster named William M. Pastore, 58, chief executive after Andrew J. McKelvey resigned his posts as chairman and chief executive. McKelvey retained his seat on the board as chairman emeritus. The company said on October 25 that it found pricing problems in a "substantial number" of its past option grants, and as a result it expected to restate its results from 1997 through

2005.

On November 22, 2006 Monster terminated Myron Olesnyckyj, the company's lead lawyer, as part of its investigation into past stock-option grant practices. In a statement, the company said Olesnyckyj was terminated "for cause."

The U.S. Attorney's Office for the Southern District of New York has issued a subpoena to the company over options backdating, and a special committee of company directors has said it wants to complete its own investigation by the end of the year. The company has delayed filing its earnings results for the second and third quarters. Second-quarter results are expected December 13. Third-quarter numbers would be issued "as soon as practicable," according to a November 7 statement from the company.

Monster Worldwide Inc. stated that it has received a notice from Nasdaq about a possible delisting of its shares due to the company's failure to file its third-quarter earnings report.

See also

- CareerBuilder
- Hotjobs
- Workopolis
- Fins.com

External links

- Official website [2]
- "The Monster.com Full Story" [3] from CareerTrainer, retrieved June 14, 2005.
- Monster Buys Affinity Labs for $61 Million [4]
- Monster Career Advice awarded a Webby Award [5]
- Ex-Monster.com CEO resigns from board over options probe [6]
- 8-K filed by Monster Worldwide with United States Securities and Exchange Commission (SEC) [7]
- SEC Filing employment agreement with CEO Bill Pastore including salary [8]
- Washington Post February 10, 2007 *Taking the Bait On a Phish Scam - Job Seekers Are Targets, Victims of Sophisticated Ploy* [9]
- Interview with CEO Jeff Taylor and COO Linda Natansohn, Onlinepersonalswatch, September 2010 [10]

Craigslist

Type	Private
Founded	1995 (incorporated 1999)
Founder	Craig Newmark
Headquarters	San Francisco Bay Area, United States
Area served	570 cities in 50 countries
Key people	Jim Buckmaster (CEO)
Services	Web Communications
Employees	32
Website	www.craigslist.org [1]
Alexa rank	33
Type of site	Classifieds, forums
Advertising	None
Registration	Optional
Available in	English, French, German, Spanish, Italian, Portuguese
Launched	1995
Current status	Active

Craigslist is a centralized network of online communities, featuring free online classified advertisements – with sections devoted to jobs, housing, personals, for sale, services, community, gigs, résumés, and discussion forums.

Craig Newmark, the founder of Craigslist, in 2006

Description

Craig Newmark began the service in 1995 as an email distribution list of friends, featuring local events in the San Francisco Bay Area, before becoming a web-based service in 1996. After incorporation as a private for-profit company in 1999, Craigslist expanded into nine more U.S. cities in 2000, four in 2001 and 2002 each, and 14 in 2003.

In 2009, Craigslist operated with a staff of 28 people. Its main source of revenue is paid job ads in select cities – $75 per ad for the San Francisco Bay Area; $25 per ad for New York City, Los Angeles, San Diego, Boston, Seattle, Washington D.C., Chicago, Philadelphia, Orange County (California) and Portland, Oregon – and paid broker apartment listings in New York City ($10 per ad).

The site serves over twenty billion page views per month, putting it in 33rd place overall among web sites worldwide and 7th place overall among web sites in the United States (per Alexa.com on June 28, 2010), with over 49.4 million unique monthly visitors in the United States alone (per Compete.com on January 8, 2010). With over eighty million new classified advertisements each month, Craigslist is the leading classifieds service in any medium. The site receives over two million new job listings each month, making it one of the top job boards in the world. The classified advertisements range from traditional buy/sell ads and community announcements to personal ads. Advertisements for "adult" (previously "erotic") services were initially given special treatment, then closed entirely on September 4, 2010, following a controversy over claims by state attorneys general that the advertisements promoted prostitution.

The site is notable for having undergone only minor design changes since its inception; even by 1996 standards, the design is very simple. Since 2001, the site design has remained virtually unchanged, and as of April 2010, Craigslist continues to avoid using images and uses only minimal CSS and JavaScript, a design philosophy common in the late 1990s but almost unheard of today for a major website.[citation needed]

In December 2006, at the UBS Global Media Conference in New York, Craigslist CEO Jim Buckmaster told Wall Street analysts that Craigslist has little interest in maximizing profit, instead it prefers to help users find cars, apartments, jobs, and dates.

The company does not formally disclose financial or ownership information. Analysts and commentators have reported varying figures for its annual revenue, ranging from $10 million in 2004, $20 million in 2005, and $25 million in 2006 to possibly $150 million in 2007. It is believed to be owned principally by Newmark, Buckmaster, and eBay (the three board members). eBay owns approximately 25%, and Newmark is believed to own the largest stake.

Background

Having observed people helping one another in friendly, social and trusting communal ways on the Internet via the WELL, MindVox and Usenet, and feeling isolated as a relative newcomer to San Francisco, Craigslist founder Craig Newmark decided to create something similar for local events.

The first emailed San Francisco event listings debuted in early 1995. The initial technology encountered some limits, so by June 1995 majordomo had been installed and the mailing list "Craigslist" resumed operations. Most of the early postings were submitted by Newmark and were notices of social events of interest to software and Internet developers living and working in San Francisco.

Craigslist headquarters in the Sunset District of San Francisco

Soon, word of mouth led to rapid growth. The number of subscribers and postings grew rapidly. There was no moderation and Newmark was surprised when people started using the mailing list for non-event postings.[citation needed] People trying to get technical positions filled found that the list was a good way to reach people with the skills they were looking for. This led to the addition of a category for "jobs". User demand for more categories caused the list of categories to grow. Community members started asking for a web interface. In need of a domain name for this, Craig registered "craigslist.org".

By early 1998, Newmark still thought his career was as a software engineer ("hardcore java programmer") and that Craigslist was a cool hobby that was getting him invited to the best parties for geeks and nerds.[citation needed] In the fall of 1998, the name "List Foundation" was introduced and Craigslist started transitioning to the use of this name. In April 1999, when Newmark learned of other organizations called "List Foundation", the use of this name was dropped. Around the time of these events, Newmark realized that the site was growing so fast that he could stop working as a software engineer and work full time running Craigslist. By April 2000, there were nine employees working out of Newmark's apartment in San Francisco.

Newmark says that Craigslist works because it gives people a voice, a sense of community trust and even intimacy. Other factors he cites are consistency of down-to-earth values, customer service and simplicity. Newmark was approached with an offer for running banner ads on Craigslist, but he decided to decline. In 2002, Craigslist staff posted mock-banner ads throughout the site as an April Fools' Day joke.

Flagging

Craigslist has a user flagging system to quickly identify illegal and inappropriate postings. Classified ad flagging does not require account log in or registration, and can be made anonymously by any visitor. When a certain number of users flag a posting, it is removed. The number of flaggings required for a posting's removal is variable and remains unknown to all but craigslist.org. Items are flagged for three categories: misplaced, prohibited, or spam/overpost. Although users are given a short description of each flagging category, users ultimately flag on their preference, prejudice, or misunderstanding of the Craigslist Terms of Use. Flaggings can also occur as acts of disruptive vandalism and for the removal of competitors postings. To better understand and clarify flagging it is up to the users to define rules themselves in such places as the Unofficial Flagging FAQ and the flag help forum. The Flag Help Forum is an unmoderated volunteer community, it is not staffed by craigslist employees, and it is not affiliated with craigslist.org. The forum volunteers have no access to information about craigslist.org user accounts or ads, and must rely upon information supplied by the ad poster to try and piece together the reason an ad was flagged and removed. The Flag Help Forum's unmoderated format allows anyone, including disruptive trolls, to post anonymously and without accountability. The forums usefulness and effectiveness can be compromised by trolls who post malicious replies to help threads.

Significant events

- In January 2000, current CEO Jim Buckmaster joined the company as lead programmer and CTO. Buckmaster contributed the site's multi-city architecture, search engine, discussion forums, flagging system, self-posting process, homepage design, personals categories, and best-of-Craigslist feature. He was promoted to CEO in November 2000.

- In 2002, a disclaimer was put on the "men seeking men", "casual encounters", "erotic services", and "rants and raves" boards to ensure that those who clicked on these sections were over the age of 18, but no disclaimer was put on the "men seeking women", "women seeking men" or "women seeking women" boards. As a response to charges of discrimination and negative stereotyping, Buckmaster explained that the company's policy is a response to user feedback requesting the warning on the more sexually explicit sections, including "men seeking men." Today, all of the above listed boards (as well as some others) have a disclaimer.

- On August 1, 2004, Craigslist began charging $25 to post job openings on the New York and Los Angeles pages. On the same day, a new section called "Gigs" was added, where low-cost and unpaid jobs and internships can be posted free.

- On August 13, 2004, Newmark announced on his blog that auction giant eBay had purchased a 25% stake in the company from a former principal. Some fans of Craigslist have expressed concern that this development will affect the site's longtime non-commercial nature, but it remains to be seen what ramifications the change will actually have. As of September 2010, there have been no substantive changes to the usefulness or non-advertising nature of the site—no banner ads, charges for a few services provided to businesses).

- In April 2008, eBay announced it was suing Craigslist to "safeguard its four-year financial investment." eBay claimed that in January 2008, Craigslist executives took actions that "unfairly diluted eBay's economic interest by more than 10%." In response, Craigslist filed a counter-suit against eBay in May 2008 "to remedy the substantial and ongoing harm to fair competition" that Craigslist claims is constituted by eBay's actions as Craigslist shareholders.

- On May 13, 2009, Craigslist announced that it would close the *erotic services* section, replacing it with an *adult services* section to be reviewed by Craigslist employees.

- On September 4, 2010, Craigslist closed the adult services section of its website. The site replaced the adult services page link with the word "censored" in white-on-black text. On September 8, 2010, the "censored" label and its dead link to adult services was completely removed from the site.

Related media

- In 2003, Michael Ferris Gibson filmed the documentary *24 Hours on Craigslist.*

- In November 2007, Ryan J. Davis directed Jeffery Self's solo show *My Life on the Craigslist* at Off-Broadway's New World Stages. The show focuses on a young man's sexual experiences on Craigslist and was so successful that it returned to New York by popular demand in February 2008.

- In the 81st Academy Awards, host Hugh Jackman performed the opening number along with the 'Craigslist' dancers (a reference to the "recession", and hence a joke that a casting call had been put on the CraigsList instead of using the usual expensive Hollywood casting techniques).

- Nerdcore hip-hop musician Schäffer the Darklord recorded a song called "Craig's List" for his album Mark Of The Beast.

- On June 16, 2009, "Weird Al" Yankovic released a song entitled "Craigslist" which is a parody of the website, done in the style of The Doors.

Reception

- In July 2005, the *San Francisco Chronicle* criticized Craigslist for allowing ads from dog breeders, and thereby allegedly encouraging the over breeding and irresponsible selling of pit bulls in the Bay Area.

- In January 2006, the *San Francisco Bay Guardian* published an editorial criticizing Craigslist for moving into local communities and "threatening to eviscerate" local alternative newspapers. Craigslist has been compared to Wal-Mart, a multinational corporation that some feel crushes small local businesses when they move into towns and offer a huge assortment of goods at lower prices.

Nonprofit foundation

In 2001, the company started the Craigslist Foundation, a § 501(c)(3) nonprofit organization that connects people to the resources they need to strengthen communities and neighborhoods. It offers free and low cost events and online resources to promote community building at all levels. It accepts charitable donations, and rather than directly funding organizations, it produces "face-to-face events and offers online resources to help grassroots organizations get off the ground and contribute real value to the community".

Since 2004, the Craigslist Foundation has hosted an annual conference called Boot Camp, an in-person event that focuses on skills for connecting, motivating and inspiring greater community involvement and impact. Boot Camp has drawn more than 10,000 people since its inception[citation needed]. The latest Boot Camp event was held on Saturday, August 14, 2010.

The Craigslist Foundation is also the fiscal sponsor for Our Good Works, the organization that manages AllforGood.org, an application that distributes volunteer opportunities across the web and helps people get involved in their communities.

Cities

The first 14 city sites were: (entire list [2])

- March 1995: San Francisco Bay Area
- June 2000: Boston
- August 2000: Chicago, Los Angeles, New York, Portland, San Diego, Seattle, Washington, D.C.
- October 2000: Sacramento
- April 2001: Atlanta, Austin, Denver, Vancouver

Vancouver, British Columbia was the first non-U.S. city included. London was the first city outside North America.

In November 2004, Amsterdam, Bangalore, Paris, São Paulo, and Tokyo became the first cities outside primarily English-speaking countries.

As of May 2008, 500 "cities" in 50 countries have Craigslist sites. Some Craigslist sites cover large regions instead of individual metropolitan areas — for example, the U.S. states of Delaware and Wyoming, the Colorado Western Slope, the California Gold Country, and the Upper Peninsula of Michigan are among the locations with their own Craigslist sites. As of 24 September 2009, there are 695 unique Craigslist sites that can be posted to.

Languages

In March 2008, Spanish, French, Italian, German, and Portuguese became the first non-English languages supported.

See also

- Craigslist controversies and illegal activities by users

External links

- Craigslist homepage [1]
- company blog [3]
- Craigslist Foundation [4]

LinkedIn

URL	www.linkedin.com [1]
Commercial?	Yes
Type of site	Professional network service
Registration	Required
Created by	Reid Hoffman
Launched	May 2003 Mountain View, CA, USA
Alexa rank	▲ 22 (October 2010)
Revenue	$17 million (December 31, 2008 Fiscal Year)
Current status	Active

LinkedIn (pronounced /ˌlɪŋkt.ˈɪn/) is a business-oriented social networking site. Founded in December 2002 and launched in May 2003, it is mainly used for professional networking. As of 9 August 2010, LinkedIn had more than 75 million registered users, spanning more than 200 countries and territories worldwide. The site is available in English, French, German, Italian, Portuguese and Spanish.

Company information

LinkedIn's CEO is Jeff Weiner, previously a Yahoo! Inc. executive. The company was founded by Reid Hoffman and founding team members from Paypal and Socialnet.com (Allen Blue, Eric Ly, Jean-Luc Vaillant, Lee Hower, Konstantin Guericke, Stephen Beitzel, David Eves, Ian McNish, Yan Pujante, and Chris Saccheri).

Founder Reid Hoffman, previously CEO of LinkedIn, is now Chairman of the Board. Dipchand Nishar is Vice President of Products. LinkedIn is headquartered in Mountain View, California, with offices in Omaha, Chicago, New York and London. It is funded by Greylock, Sequoia Capital, Bain Capital Ventures, Bessemer Venture Partners and the European Founders Fund. LinkedIn reached profitability in March 2006.

On June 17, 2008, Sequoia Capital, Greylock Partners, and other venture capital firms purchased a 5% stake in the company for $53 million, giving the company a post-money valuation of approximately $1 billion.

In June 2010, LinkedIn announced it would be opening up a European headquarters in Dublin, Ireland.

On July 28, 2010, Tiger Global Management LLC purchased a 1% stake in the company at a valuation of approximately $2 billion.

On August 4, 2010, LinkedIn announced Mspoke acquisition. This is the company's first acquisition for an undisclosed amount. This acquisition aims to help LinkedIn users do more than just find a job, increase users' activity and improve its 1% premium subscription ratio.

LinkedIn service

Membership

With 80 million users, LinkedIn is ahead of its competitors Viadeo (30 million) and XING (9 million).The membership grows by a new member approximately every second. About half of the members are in the United States and 11 million are from Europe. With 3 million users, India is the fastest-growing country as of 2009. The Netherlands has the highest adoption rate per capita outside the US at 30%. LinkedIn recently reached 4 million users in UK and 1 million in Spain.

Features

The purpose of the site is to allow registered users to maintain a list of contact details of people they know and trust in business. The people in the list are called *Connections*. Users can invite anyone (whether a site user or not) to become a connection.

This list of connections can then be used in a number of ways:

- A contact network is built up consisting of their direct connections, the connections of each of their connections (termed *second-degree connections*) and also the connections of second-degree connections (termed *third-degree connections*). This can be used to gain an introduction to someone a person wishes to know through a mutual, trusted contact.
- It can then be used to find jobs, people and business opportunities recommended by someone in one's contact network.
- Employers can list jobs and search for potential candidates.
- Job seekers can review the profile of hiring managers and discover which of their existing contacts can introduce them.
- Users can post their own photos and view photos of others to aid in identification.
- Users can now follow different companies and can get notification about the new joining and offers available.
- Users can save (i.e. bookmark) jobs which they would like to apply for.

The "gated-access approach" (where contact with any professional requires either a preexisting relationship, or the intervention of a contact of theirs) is intended to build trust among the service's users. LinkedIn participates in EU's International Safe Harbor Privacy Principles.

LinkedIn also allows users to research companies with which they may be interested in working. When typing the name of a given company in the search box, statistics about the company are provided. These may include the ratio of female to male employees, the percentage of the most common titles/positions held within the company, the location of the company's headquarters and offices, or a list of present and former employees.

The feature LinkedIn Answers, similar to Yahoo! Answers, allows users to ask questions for the community to answer. This feature is free and the main difference from the latter is that questions are potentially more business-oriented, and the identity of the people asking and answering questions is known.

The searchable LinkedIn Groups feature allows users to establish new business relationships by joining alumni, industry, or professional and other relevant groups. LinkedIn groups can be created in any subjects and by any member of LinkedIn. Some groups are specialised groups dealing with a narrow domain or industry whereas others are very broad and generic in nature.

Another LinkedIn feature is LinkedIn Polls.

A mobile version of the site was launched in February 2008 which gives access to a reduced feature set over a mobile phone. The mobile service is available in six languages: Chinese, English, French, German, Japanese and Spanish.

In mid-2008, LinkedIn launched LinkedIn DirectAds as a form of sponsored advertising.

In October, 2008, LinkedIn revealed plans to opening its social network of 30 million professionals globally as a potential sample for business-to-business research. And, in doing so it's testing a potential social-network revenue model-research that to some appears more promising than advertising.

In October, 2008, LinkedIn enabled an "applications platform" that allows other online services to be embedded within a member's profile page. For example, among the initial applications were an Amazon Reading List that allows LinkedIn members to display books they are reading, a connection to Tripit, and a Six Apart, WordPress and TypePad application that allows members to display their latest blog postings within their LinkedIn profile.

Restricted access from some countries

In 2009 Syrian users reported that LinkedIn server stopped accepting connections originating from IP addresses assigned to Syria. As company's Customer Support stated, services provided by them are subject to US export and re-export control laws and regulations and *"As such, and as a matter of corporate policy, we do not allow member accounts or access to our site from Cuba, Iran, North Korea, Sudan, or Syria."*

Cuba, Iran, Sudan and Syria are not available in the list of countries that LinkedIn users can select as one's location. However, as of April 2010, North Korea is still present there.

SNA LinkedIn

The Search, Network, and Analytics team at LinkedIn has a web site that hosts the open source projects built by the group. The most notable one is Project Voldemort, a distributed key-value structured storage system with low-latency similar in purpose to Amazon's Dynamo and Google's BigTable.

See also

- Business network
- Information Routing Group
- LinkedIn Answers
- List of social networking websites
- Reputation systems
- Social network
- Social software

External links

- Official website [1]
- Professional networking online: A qualitative study of LinkedIn use in Norway (2008) [2] - Master thesis on how professionals in Norway use LinkedIn.

Yahoo! HotJobs

URL	www.hotjobs.yahoo.com [1]
Commercial?	Yes
Type of site	Job Search Engine
Registration	Optional
Available language(s)	Multilingual
Owner	Monster Worldwide
Created by	Richard Johnson
Launched	1996
Alexa rank	3
Current status	Active

Yahoo! HotJobs, formerly known as **hotjobs.com**, is an online job search engine. Yahoo! HotJobs provides tools and advice for job seekers, employers, and staffing firms. It was acquired by Yahoo! in 2002. It was sold to Monster.com on February 3, 2010.

History

hotjobs.com was founded by Richard Johnson and was based at 24 West 40th Street, 12th floor in New York City, just across from Bryant Park. Johnson had previously founded the RBL Agency with Ben Carroccio, a boutique employment agency for technologists. The initial website was launched in early 1996 as RBL Agency which evolved in to the Online Technical Employment Center (OTEC) in 1999, and only featured technical jobs. Founding employees Christopher G. Stach II, Earle Ady, and Allen Murabayashi designed and coded the first iterations of the site on Silicon Graphics Indy workstations for C application development, Apple Macs for content creation, and the site ran on Sun and SGI hardware.

The company's first advertising effort was as a Yahoo! site of the week, which at the time could be purchased for $1000.

hotjobs participated in one of Jupiter Communications' first conferences at the New York Sheraton in February 1996. It was here that Johnson spotted Ginna Basinger, who was working for the Sheraton at the time, and offered her a position as the first hotjobs sales person. The product was given away to the first 100+ clients to gain employment content to attract job seekers.

Thomas Chin joined the organization in October 1996 while attending Columbia University, and eventually became the organization's chief scientist.

In the summer of 1997, Johnson decided to expand the operations, and brought a number of recruiters over from the RBL Agency to join the salesforce. Dimitri Boylan joined at this time heading up the sales and marketing effort. Over Labor Day weekend in 1997, the first remote sales office was opened in Burlingame, CA by Earle, Kelly Michaelian & Michael Tjoa. This was a joint venture between hotjobs & otec. Ginna Basinger moved from New York to California to manage the office, hiring the company's first non-New York employee, Michael Johnson, in August 1997 as an Account Executive. Quickly outgrowing the space, the Burlingame office was moved to downtown San Francisco in the Summer of 1999 where it remained through the disposition of the company in 2002.

hotjobs developed "softshoe" a private label job board and applicant tracking system in 1997. Lucent Technologies was the first client of this product.

In September 1997, hotjobs shed the technology-only focus by adding job categories for "Finance/Accounting" and "Sales/Marketing." The first hotjobs newsletter followed in October 1997. During this time the name was also officially changed from "HotJobs, Inc." to "HotJobs.com, Ltd" on the suggestion of Peter Connors, who had been hired as the first marketing manager.

The company startled the advertising world in 1999 when it bought a $1.6 million commercial during Super Bowl XXXIII, considering that its total revenues were approximately $2.5 million. McCann-Erickson Detroit was hired for the production. It proved to be a very savvy investment, as over $25 million in publicity was generated as a consequence. Immediately following the playing of the commercial, hotjobs' servers were overwhelmed with requests, and this incident later served as the basis for a commercial for IBM. [citation needed] The company went public in late 1999.

In 2000, the company had grown to $100 million dollars in revenue and moved its headquarters to 406 West 31st Street. The company expanded into the enterprise market by purchasing the distressed resume processing company Resumix, Inc. of Sunnyvale, Ca. As part of this effort, the company hired Tim Villanueva, formerly a leading developer at Intuit, as its Chief Technology Officer, and Chuck Price, formerly Chief Architect at Broadvision, as its Senior VP of Engineering. Allen and Thomas left shortly after this leadership expansion to pursue new interests.

In March 2001, Richard Johnson resigned as Chief Executive Officer and President. The board appointed COO Dimitri Boylan to fill those positions. In 2001 the company became profitable and cash flow positive.

Yahoo! purchased the company through an unsolicited bid in 2002, for $436 million, undercutting efforts by Monster.com to acquire the company. However, Monster.com announced in February 2010 that it would acquire HotJobs from Yahoo for $225 million dollars. Yahoo and Monster as a part of a deal, also agreed to a three-year traffic sharing agreement where Yahoo will promote Monster as its official job listings site in exchange for receiving a share of the site's profits.

Concept

Yahoo! HotJobs' services are free to job seeking users and include posting up to ten versions of a resume. Once signed on, job searches can be saved, allowing ongoing results to be emailed to the user. Job seekers have the ability to pull up statistics that feature the number of times an employer/recruiter reviewed their resume and a complete history of sent cover letters and resumes. Various tools within the site allow users to calculate ideal salaries, research plans and employee stock options as well as have a "Job Tip of the Day" emailed to them. The Career Tools tab lists other items they offer, like resume building, interviewing advice and an education center. Additionally, using the "HotBlock" feature, applicants can block some or all of HotJobs' companies from viewing their resumes.

Yahoo! HotJobs provides employers access to their resume search engine and the ability to post, edit and delete job ads at anytime and as often as they like at no additional cost. Employers are given access to a variety of communication devices, including letter templates and notes, as well as the ability to track their postings.

Awards

Job seekers voted Yahoo! Hotjobs the (2002, 2003) "Best General Purpose Job Board for Job Seekers," and recruiters voted Yahoo! HotJobs the (2003) "Most Recruiter-Friendly General Purpose Site" in a survey conducted by WEDDLE's.

See also

- Monster.com
- Simply Hired
- Indeed.com
- CareerBuilder
- Fins.com

External links

- Yahoo! HotJobs Official website [1]

References

- Wired 8.02: Hot Spots! [2]
- ZDNET [3]

Simply Hired

URL	www.SimplyHired.com [1]
Commercial?	Yes
Type of site	Job Search Engine
Available language(s)	English, German, French, Spanish, Dutch, Italian, Portuguese, Japanese
Current status	Active

Simply Hired is a metasearch engine for job listings (thus also an example of vertical search) and online recruitment advertising network. The company aggregates job listings from thousands of sites across the Web including job boards, newspaper and classified listings, associations, social networks, content sites and company career sites. It then distributes those jobs on SimplyHired.com, and its 5,000 social network, media content, blog, and niche website partners. Advertisers can gain premium placement across its network through advertising in a pay-per-click (PPC) model. Job seekers search job listings on SimplyHired.com by keyword and location to find jobs of interest. Clicking a job title will take the user directly to the source site with the full job description and instructions for applying. Simply Hired currently operates job search engines in 17 countries: Australia, Belgium, Brazil, Canada, France, Germany, India, Ireland, Italy, Japan, Mexico, the Netherlands, Switzerland, China, Spain, the United Kingdom, and the United States.

History

Simply Hired, Inc. was founded in 2003 by Gautam Godhwani and Peter Weck and the initial beta site launch occurred on March 16, 2005. In April 2006, the company received US$13.5 million in funding from News Corp.'s Fox Interactive Media division. The company partnered with MySpace Careers in June 2006 to power the website. Simply Hired partnered with *The Washington Post* in March 2009 to provide job listings on the newspaper's website. The company raised another $4.6 million in August 2009 from IDG Ventures.

As of August 2009, the company has raised $22.3M in funding from IDG Ventures SF, News Corporation's Fox Interactive Media, Foundation Capital, Garage Technology Ventures and individual investors and founders including most recently $4.6M of new investment funding from IDG Ventures and Foundation Capital. The founders themselves invested $1.2M in the company.

Services

Services include job search, job trends, salary search, local jobs, recruitment advertising, and publisher programs.

See also

- Employment website
- Indeed.com
- LinkUp (website)
- Fins.com

External links

- SimplyHired.com [2]
- Simply Hired Company Blog [3]
- Simply Hired Publisher Network [4]
- Simply Hired [5] at CrunchBase

Indeed.com

URL	www.indeed.com [1]
Commercial?	Yes
Type of site	Job Search Engine
Available language(s)	Chinese, Czech, Danish, Dutch, English, Finnish, French, German, Greek, Hebrew, Hungarian, Italian, Japanese, Korean, Malay, Norwegian Bokmål, Polish, Portuguese, Romanian, Russian, Spanish, Swedish, Turkish
Current status	Active

Indeed.com is a metasearch engine for job listings, launched in November 2004. As a single-topic search engine, it is also an example of vertical search. The site aggregates job listings from thousands of websites including job boards, newspapers, associations, and company career pages. Job seekers do not apply for jobs through Indeed, just receive the listing as to where the job is posted. Applicants can then decide which jobs are of interest and then go to the corresponding sites to apply. Indeed is currently available in 54 countries, Antarctica, Argentina, Australia, Austria, Bahrain, Belgium, Brazil, Canada, Chile, China, Colombia, Czech Republic, Denmark, Finland, France, Germany, Greece, Hong Kong, Hungary, India, Indonesia, Ireland, Israel, Italy, Japan, Korea, Kuwait, Luxembourg, Malaysia, Mexico, Netherlands, New Zealand, Norway, Oman, Pakistan, Peru, Philippines, Poland, Portugal, Qatar, Romania, Russia, Saudi Arabia, Singapore, South Africa, Spain, Sweden, Switzerland, Taiwan, Turkey, United Arab Emirates, the UK, the USA, and Venezuela. After April 1, 2010, Indeed was the first site available in 7 continents.

History

Indeed was co-founded by Paul Forster and Rony Kahan. The company is privately held with investment from The New York Times Company, Allen & Company and Union Square Ventures.

In 2005, Indeed launched their beta version of what they refer to as "pay-per-click job advertising network". In addition to searching job postings, it also allows the occurrence of words therein to be plotted over time, ostensibly as an indicator of trends in the job market.

Services

Services include job search, job trends, industry trends, salary search, job competition index, and website forums.

See also

- Employment website
- Monster
- CareerBuilder
- Simply Hired
- LinkUp (website)
- Fins.com

External links

- Indeed.com [1]
- Indeed Company Blog [2]

FINS.com

URL	http://www.fins.com/
Slogan	"Propel Your Career"
Commercial?	Yes
Type of site	Job Search and Career Management Resource
Registration	Optional
Available language(s)	English
Owner	Dow Jones & Company
Launched	2009
Current status	Active

FINS.com is a standalone resource for financial professionals with information about finance careers and the finance industry, launched in July 2009 by Dow Jones & Company, publisher of The Wall Street Journal. The site's products and services include a job search engine, the FINS Sector Index[1] of information about sectors within the finance industry including accounting, capital markets, hedge funds, private equity/venture capital and wealth management, and information on more than 1,500 companies in financial services

FINS has an editorial staff that writes Morning Coffee, "which summarizes the news from the financial world and its likely impact on the hiring market," and the Bull/Bear Report, "which tracks industry job openings."

History

Founded in 2009, FINS.com is part of The Wall Street Journal Digital Network, which includes WSJ.com[2], MarketWatch.com[3], Barrons.com[4] and AllThingsD.com[5].

Services

Services include job search, job trends, industry trends, company research, career management tips, job search tips, the FINS Resume Service, Morning Coffee, the Bull/Bear Report and FINSWire.

See Also

- CareerBuilder
- Hotjobs
- Monster.com
- Simply Hired
- Indeed.com

External links

- Official website [6]
- FINS Blog [7]

Connect on Facebook and Twitter

Twitter

Type	Private
Founded	San Francisco, California, United States
Founder	Jack Dorsey Evan Williams Biz Stone
Headquarters	795 Folsom St., Suite 600, San Francisco, CA 94107, United States
Area served	Worldwide
Key people	Jack Dorsey (Chairman) Dick Costolo (CEO) Evan Williams (Product Strategy) Biz Stone (Creative Director)
Revenue	▲ US $150 million (projected 2010)
Employees	300 (2010)
Slogan	What's happening?
Website	twitter.com [1]
Alexa rank	▲ 9 (October 2010)
Type of site	mobile social network service, microblogging
Registration	Required
Users	190 million (visitors monthly)
Available in	Multilingual English, Spanish, Japanese, German, French, and Italian
Launched	July 15, 2006
Current status	Active

Twitter is a website, owned and operated by Twitter Inc., which offers a social networking and microblogging service, enabling its users to send and read other users' messages called *tweets*. Tweets are text-based posts of up to 140 characters displayed on the user's profile page. Tweets are publicly visible by default, however senders can restrict message delivery to their friends list. Users may subscribe to other author tweets—this is known as *following* and subscribers are known as *followers*. As of late 2009, users can follow lists of authors instead of just following individual authors.

All users can send and receive tweets via the Twitter website, compatible external applications (such as for smartphones), or by Short Message Service (SMS) available in certain countries. While the service is free, accessing it through SMS may incur phone service provider fees. The website is based in San Bruno, California near San Francisco (where the website was first based). Twitter also has servers and offices in San Antonio, Texas and Boston, Massachusetts.

Since its creation in 2006 by Jack Dorsey, Twitter has gained popularity worldwide and currently has more than 100 million users. It is sometimes described as the "SMS of the Internet."

History

Twitter's origins lie in a "daylong brainstorming session" that was held by board members of the podcasting company Odeo. During the meeting, Jack Dorsey introduced the idea of an individual using an SMS service to communicate with a small group. The original project code name for the service was **twttr**, inspired by Flickr and the five character length of American SMS short codes. The developers initially considered "10958" as a short code, but later changed it to "40404" for "ease of use and memorability." Work on the project started on March 21, 2006, when Dorsey published the first Twitter message at 9:50 PM Pacific Standard Time (PST): "just setting up my twttr."

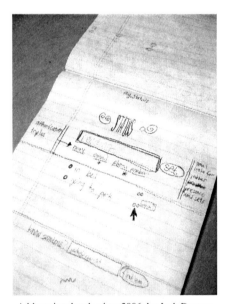

A blueprint sketch, circa 2006, by Jack Dorsey, envisioning an SMS-based social network.

> [W]e came across the word "twitter," and it was just perfect. The definition was "a short burst of inconsequential information," and "chirps from birds." And that's exactly what the product was.

—Jack Dorsey

The first Twitter prototype was used as an internal service for Odeo employees and the full version was introduced publicly on July 15, 2006. In October 2006, Biz Stone, Evan Williams, Dorsey, and other members of Odeo formed Obvious Corporation and acquired Odeo and all of its assets—including

Odeo.com and Twitter.com—from the investors and shareholders. Twitter spun off into its own company in April 2007.

The tipping point for Twitter's popularity was the 2007 South by Southwest (SXSW) festival. During the event Twitter usage increased from 20,000 tweets per day to 60,000. "The Twitter people cleverly placed two 60-inch plasma screens in the conference hallways, exclusively streaming Twitter messages," remarked *Newsweek's* Steven Levy. "Hundreds of conference-goers kept tabs on each other via constant twitters. Panelists and speakers mentioned the service, and the bloggers in attendance touted it."

Reaction at the festival was highly positive. Blogger Scott Beale said that Twitter "absolutely rul[ed]" SXSW. Social software researcher Danah Boyd said Twitter "own[ed]" the festival. Twitter staff received the festival's Web Award prize with the remark "we'd like to thank you in 140 characters or less. And we just did!"

On September 14, 2010, Twitter launched a redesigned site including a new logo.

On October 4, 2010, Evan Williams announced that he was stepping down as CEO. Dick Costolo, formerly COO of Twitter, took over Williams' position. Williams will stay with the company and "be completely focused on product strategy."

Previous Twitter logo, used until September 14, 2010.

Growth

Twitter had 400,000 tweets posted per quarter in 2007. This grew to 100 million tweets posted per quarter in 2008. By the end of 2009, 2 billion tweets per quarter were being posted. [citation needed] By March 2010, Twitter recorded over 70,000 registered applications, according to the company. In February 2010 Twitter users were sending 50 million tweets per day. In the first quarter of 2010, 4 billion tweets were posted. [citation needed] As of June 2010, about 65 million tweets are posted each day, equalling about 750 tweets sent each second, according to Twitter.

Twitter's usage spikes during prominent events. For example, a record was set during the 2010 FIFA World Cup when fans wrote 2,940 tweets per second in the 30 second period after Japan scored against Cameroon on 14 June 2010. The record was broken again when 3,085 tweets a second were posted after the Los Angeles Lakers' victory in the 2010 NBA Finals on 17 June 2010. When American singer Michael Jackson died on June 25, 2009, the Twitter server crashed after users were updating their status to include the words "Michael Jackson" at a rate of 100,000 tweets per hour.

Twitter acquired application developer Atebits on April 11, 2010. Atebits had developed the Apple Design Award-winning Twitter client Tweetie for Mac and iPhone. The application, now called "Twitter" and distributed free of charge, is the official Twitter client for the iPhone.

Overview

Technology author Steven Johnson describes the basic mechanics of Twitter as "remarkably simple:"

> As a social network, Twitter revolves around the principle of followers. When you choose to follow another Twitter user, that user's tweets appear in reverse chronological order on your main Twitter page. If you follow 20 people, you'll see a mix of tweets scrolling down the page: breakfast-cereal updates, interesting new links, music recommendations, even musings on the future of education.

Twitter has been compared to a web-based Internet Relay Chat (IRC) client.

Messages

Users can group posts together by topic or type by use of *hashtags* — words or phrases prefixed with a #. Similarly, the letter d followed by a username allows users to send messages privately. Finally, the @ sign followed by a username is used for mentioning or replying to other users.

In late 2009, the "Twitter Lists" feature was added, making it possible for users to follow (as well as mention and reply to) lists of authors instead of individual authors.

Through SMS, users can communicate with Twitter through five gateway numbers: short codes for the United States, Canada, India, New Zealand, and an Isle of Man-based number for international use. There is also a short code in the United Kingdom which is only accessible to those on the Vodafone, O2 and Orange networks. In India, since Twitter only supports tweets from Bharti Airtel, an alternative platform called smsTweet was set up by a user to work on all networks. A similar platform called GladlyCast exists for mobile phone users in Singapore, Malaysia and the Philippines.

The messages were initially set to 140-character limit for compatibility with SMS messaging, introducing the shorthand notation and slang commonly used in SMS messages. The 140 character limit has also increased the usage of URL shortening services such as bit.ly, goo.gl, and tr.im, and content hosting services, such as Twitpic, memozu.com and NotePub to accommodate multimedia content and text longer than 140 characters. Twitter uses bit.ly for automatic shortening of all URLs posted on its website.

Tweet contents

San Antonio-based market research firm Pear Analytics analyzed 2,000 tweets (originating from the US and in English) over a 2-week period in August 2009 from 11:00a to 5:00p (CST) and separated them into six categories:

- Pointless babble — 41%
- Conversational — 38%
- Pass-along value — 9%
- Self-promotion — 6%
- Spam — 4%
- News — 4%

Social networking researcher Danah Boyd responded to the Pear Analytics survey by arguing that what the Pear researchers labelled "pointless babble" is better characterized as "social grooming" and/or "peripheral awareness" (which she explains as persons "want[ing] to know what the people around them are thinking and doing and feeling, even when co-presence isn't viable").

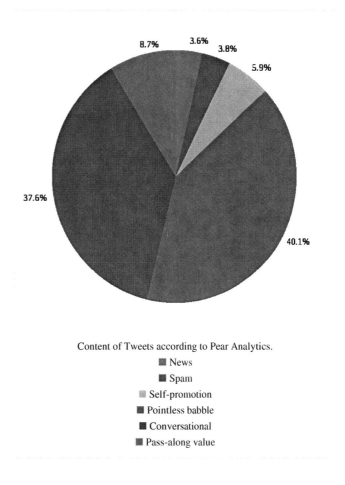

Content of Tweets according to Pear Analytics.
- News
- Spam
- Self-promotion
- Pointless babble
- Conversational
- Pass-along value

Rankings

Twitter is ranked as one of the 10 most visited websites worldwide by Alexa's web traffic analysis. Daily user estimates vary because the company does not release the number of active accounts. A February 2009 Compete.com blog entry ranked Twitter as the third most used social network based on their count of 6 million unique monthly visitors and 55 million monthly visits. In March 2009, a Nielsen.com blog ranked Twitter as the fastest-growing website in the Member Communities category for February 2009. Twitter had a monthly growth of 1,382%, increasing from 475,000 unique visitors in February 2008 to 7 million in February 2009. It was followed by Zimbio with 240% increase, and Facebook with 228% increase. However, only 40% of Twitter's users are retained.

Adding and following content

There are numerous tools for adding content, monitoring content and conversations including Tweetdeck, Salesforce.com, HootSuite, and Twitterfeed. Less than half of tweets are posted using the web user interface with most users using third-party applications (based on analysis of 500 million tweets by Sysomos).

Authentication

As of August 31, 2010, third-party Twitter applications are required to use OAuth, an authentication method that allows users to use applications without having to give the applications their passwords. Previously, this authentication method was optional, but now third-party applications that try to use a username and password will fail. Twitter stated that the move to OAuth will mean "increased security and a better experience."

Demographics

Twitter is mainly used by older adults who might not have used other social sites before Twitter, says Jeremiah Owyang, an industry analyst studying social media. "Adults are just catching up to what teens have been doing for years," he said. According to comScore only 11% of Twitter's users are aged 12 to 17. comScore attributes this to Twitter's "early adopter period" when the social network first gained popularity in business settings and news outlets attracting primarily older users. However, comScore as of late, has stated that Twitter has begun to "filter more into the mainstream", and "along with it came a culture of celebrity as Shaq, Britney Spears and Ashton Kutcher joined the ranks of the Twitterati."

According to a study by Sysomos in June 2009, women make up a slightly larger Twitter demographic than men — 53% over 47%. It also stated that 5% of users accounted for 75% of all activity, and that New York has the most Twitter users.

According to Quancast, 27 million people in the US used Twitter as of 09/03/2009. 63% of Twitter users are less than 35 years old, 60% of Twitter users are Caucasian, but a higher than average (compared to other Internet properties) are African American (16%) and Hispanic (11%); 58% of Twitter users have a total household income of at least $60K.

Finances

Twitter raised over US$57 million from venture capitalist growth funding, although exact numbers are not publicly disclosed. Twitter's first A round of funding was for an undisclosed amount that is rumored to have been between $1 million and $5 million. Its second B round of funding in 2008 was for $22 million and its third C round of funding in 2009 was for $35 million from Institutional Venture Partners and Benchmark Capital along with an undisclosed amount from other investors including Union Square Ventures, Spark Capital and Insight Venture Partners. Twitter is backed by Union Square Ventures, Digital Garage, Spark Capital, and Bezos Expeditions.

Twitter's San Francisco headquarters located at 795 Folsom St.

The Industry Standard has remarked that Twitter's long-term viability is limited by a lack of revenue. Twitter board member Todd Chaffee forecast that the company could profit from e-commerce, noting that users may want to buy items directly from Twitter since it already provides product recommendations and promotions.

On April 13, 2010, Twitter announced plans to offer paid advertising for companies that would be able to purchase "promoted tweets" to appear in selective search results on the Twitter website, similar to Google Adwords' advertising model. As of April 13, Twitter announced it had already signed up a number of companies wishing to advertise including Sony Pictures, Red Bull, Best Buy, and Starbucks.

Some of Twitter's revenue and user growth documents were illegally published on TechCrunch by the hacker Croll Hacker. The documents projected 2009 revenues of $400,000 in the third quarter and $4 million in the fourth quarter along with 25 million users by the end of the year. The projections for the end of 2013 were $1.54 billion in revenue, $111 million in net earnings, and 1 billion users. No information about how Twitter plans to achieve those numbers has been published. In response, Twitter co-founder Biz Stone published a blog post suggesting the possibility of legal action against the hacker.

Technology

Implementation

The Twitter Web interface uses the Ruby on Rails framework, deployed on a performance enhanced Ruby Enterprise Edition implementation of Ruby.

From the spring of 2007 until 2008 the messages were handled by a Ruby persistent queue server called Starling, but since 2009 implementation has been gradually replaced with software written in Scala. The service's application programming interface (API) allows other web services and applications to integrate with Twitter.

Interface

On April 30, 2009, Twitter adjusted its web interface, adding a search bar and a sidebar of "trending topics" — the most common phrases appearing in messages. Biz Stone explains that all messages are instantly indexed and that "with this newly launched feature, Twitter has become something unexpectedly important — a discovery engine for finding out what is happening right now."

Outages

When Twitter experiences an outage, users see the "fail whale" error message image created by Yiying Lu, illustrating several red birds using a net to hoist a whale from the ocean captioned "Too many tweets! Please wait a moment and try again."

Twitter had approximately 98% uptime in 2007 (or about six full days of downtime). The downtime was particularly noticeable during events popular with the technology industry such as the 2008 Macworld Conference & Expo keynote address.

* May 2008 Twitter's new engineering team made architectural changes to deal with the scale of growth. Stability issues resulted in down time or temporary feature removal.

* August 2008, Twitter withdrew free SMS services from users in the United Kingdom and for approximately five months instant messaging support via a XMPP bot was listed as being "temporarily unavailable".

* October 10, 2008, Twitter's status blog announced that instant messaging (IM) service was no longer a temporary outage and needed to be revamped. It was announced that Twitter aims to return its IM service pending necessary major work.

* June 12, 2009, in what was called a potential "Twitpocalypse", the unique numerical identifier associated with each tweet exceeded the limit of 32-bit signed integers (2,147,483,647 total messages). While Twitter itself was not affected, some third-party clients could no longer access recent tweets. Patches were quickly released, though some iPhone applications had to wait for approval from the App Store.

- September 22, the identifier exceeded the limit for 32-bit *unsigned* integers (4,294,967,296 total messages) again breaking some third-party clients.

- August 6, 2009, Twitter and Facebook suffered from a denial-of-service attack, causing the Twitter website to go offline for several hours. It was later confirmed that the attacks were directed at one pro-Georgian user around the anniversary of the 2008 South Ossetia War, rather than the sites themselves.

- 17 December 2009 a hacking attack replaced the website's welcoming screen with an image of a green flag and the caption "This site has been hacked by Iranian Cyber Army" for nearly an hour. No connection between the hackers and Iran has been established.

Privacy and security

Twitter collects personally identifiable information about its users and shares it with third parties. The service reserves the right to sell this information as an asset if the company changes hands. While Twitter displays no advertising, advertisers can target users based on their history of tweets and may quote tweets in ads directed specifically to the user.

A security vulnerability was reported on April 7, 2007, by Nitesh Dhanjani and Rujith. Since Twitter used the phone number of the sender of an SMS message as authentication, malicious users could update someone else's status page by using SMS spoofing. The vulnerability could be used if the spoofer knew the phone number registered to their victim's account. Within a few weeks of this discovery Twitter introduced an optional personal identification number (PIN) that its users could use to authenticate their SMS-originating messages.

On January 5, 2009, 33 high-profile Twitter accounts were compromised after a Twitter administrator's password was guessed by a dictionary attack. Falsified tweets — including sexually explicit and drug-related messages — were sent from these accounts.

Twitter launched the beta version of their "Verified Accounts" service on June 11, 2009, allowing famous or notable people to announce their Twitter account name. The home pages of these accounts display a badge indicating their status.

In May 2010, a bug was discovered by İnci Sözlük users that allowed Twitter users to force others to follow them without the other user's knowledge. For example, comedian Conan O'Brien's account which had been set to follow only one person was changed to receive nearly 200 malicious subscriptions.

In response to Twitter's security breaches, the Federal Trade Commission brought charges against the service which were settled on June 24, 2010. This was the first time the FTC had taken action against a social network for security lapses. The settlement requires Twitter to take a number of steps to secure users' private information including maintenance of a "comprehensive information security program" to be independently audited biannually.

"MouseOver" exploit

On 21 September 2010, an XSS Worm became active on Twitter. When an account user held the mouse cursor over blacked out parts of a tweet, the worm within the script would automatically open links and re-post itself on the reader's account. The exploit was then re-used to post pop-up ads and links to pornographic sites.

The origin is unclear but Pearce Delphin (known on Twitter as @zzap) and a Scandinavian developer, Magnus Holm, both claim to have modified the exploit of a user, possibly Masato Kinugawa, who was using it to create coloured Tweets. Kinugawa, a Japanese developer, reported the XSS vulnerability to Twitter on August 14. Later, when he found it was exploitable again, he created the account 'RainbowTwtr' and used it to post coloured messages.

Delphin says he exposed the security flaw by tweeting a JavaScript function for "onMouseOver", and Holm later created and posted the XSS Worm that automatically re-tweeted itself.

Accounts affected by the virus included Sarah Brown, wife of former British Prime Minister Gordon Brown. Security firm Sophos reported the virus was spread by people doing it for "fun and games", but noted it could be exploited by cybercriminals. Twitter issued a statement on their status blog at 13:50 UTC that "*The exploit is fully patched*". Twitter representative Carolyn Penner has expressed that they will not be pressing charges over this incident.

Open source

Twitter released several open source projects developed while overcoming technical challenges of their service. Notable projects are the Gizzard Scala framework for creating distributed datastores and the distributed graph database FlockDB.

t.co

t.co is a URL shortening service created by Twitter. It is only available for links posted to Twitter and not available for general use. Eventually all links posted to Twitter will use a t.co wrapper.

Twitter hopes that the service will be able to protect users from malicious sites, and will use it to track clicks on links within tweets.

History

Having previously used the services of third parties TinyURL and bit.ly, Twitter began experimenting with its own URL shortening service for direct messages in March 2010 using the twt.tl domain, before it purchased the t.co domain.

The service is being tested on the main site using the accounts @TwitterAPI, @rsarver and @raffi.

On 2 September 2010 an email from Twitter to users said they would be expanding the roll-out of the service to users.

Reception

Change of focus

Twitter emphasized their news and information network strategy in November 2009 by changing the question asked users for status updates from "What are you doing?" to "What's happening?". *Entertainment Weekly* put it on its end-of-the-decade, "best-of" list, saying, "Limiting yourself to 140 characters—the maximum for messages on this diabolically addictive social-networking tool—is easy."

Criticism

The Wall Street Journal wrote that social-networking services such as Twitter "elicit mixed feelings in the technology-savvy people who have been their early adopters. Fans say they are a good way to keep in touch with busy friends. But some users are starting to feel 'too' connected, as they grapple with check-in messages at odd hours, higher cellphone bills and the need to tell acquaintances to stop announcing what they're having for dinner."

"Using Twitter for literate communication is about as likely as firing up a CB radio and hearing some guy recite the *Iliad*", said tech writer Bruce Sterling. "For many people, the idea of describing your blow-by-blow activities in such detail is absurd," hypothesized writer Clive Thompson. "Why would you subject your friends to your daily minutiae? And conversely, how much of their trivia can you absorb? The growth of ambient intimacy can seem like modern narcissism taken to a new, supermetabolic extreme—the ultimate expression of a generation of celebrity-addled youths who believe their every utterance is fascinating and ought to be shared with the world."

On the other hand Steve Dotto opines that part of Twitter's appeal is the challenge of trying to publish such messages in tight constraints. "The qualities that make Twitter seem inane and half-baked are what makes it so powerful," says Jonathan Zittrain, professor of Internet law at Harvard Law School.

Nielsen Online reports that Twitter has a user retention rate of 40%. Many people stop using the service after a month therefore the site may potentially reach only about 10% of all Internet users. In 2009, Twitter won the "Breakout of the Year" Webby Award.

During a February 2009 discussion on National Public Radio's *Weekend Edition*, Daniel Schorr stated that Twitter accounts of events lacked rigorous fact-checking and other editorial improvements. In response, Andy Carvin gave Schorr two examples of breaking news stories that played out on Twitter and said users wanted first-hand accounts and sometimes debunked stories.

In an episode of *The Daily Show* on February 26, 2009, guest Brian Williams described tweets as only referring to the condition of the author. Williams implied that he would never use Twitter because nothing he did was interesting enough to publish in Twitter format. During another episode of *The Daily Show* on March 2, 2009, host Jon Stewart negatively portrayed members of Congress who chose to "tweet" during President Obama's address to Congress (on February 24, 2009) rather than pay attention to the content of the speech. The show's Samantha Bee satirized media coverage of the service saying "there's no surprise young people love it — according to reports of young people by middle-aged people."

In March 2009, the comic strip *Doonesbury* began to satirize Twitter. Many characters highlighted the triviality of tweets although one defended the need to keep up with the constant-update trend. SuperNews! similarly satirized Twitter as an addiction to "constant self-affirmation" and said tweets were nothing more than "shouts into the darkness hoping someone is listening".

In August 2010, South Korea tried to block Twitter due to the North Korean government opening a Twitter account. The North Korean Twitter account created on August 12, @uriminzok, loosely translated to mean "our people" in Korean, acquired over 4,500 followers in less than one week. On August 19, 2010, South Korea's state-run Communications Standards Commission banned the Twitter account for broadcasting "illegal information." According to BBC US and Canada, experts claim that North Korea has invested in "information technology for more than 20 years" with knowledge of how to use social networking sites to their power This appears to be "nothing new" for North Korea as the reclusive country has always published propaganda in its press, usually against South Korea, calling them "warmongers." With only 36 tweets, the Twitter account was able to accumulate almost 9,000 followers. To date, the South Korean Commission has banned 65 sites, including this Twitter account.

See also

- Ambient Awareness
- Comparison of micro-blogging services
- List of Twitter services and applications

External links

- Official website [1]
- Twitter [2] on Twitter
- Twitter Demographics and Audience Profile [3] at Quantcast

- Twitter in Depth Archive [4] by *The Daily Telegraph*
- The Library of Congress is Archiving Your Tweets [5] – audio report by *NPR*
- Twittermania sweeps Russia's politicians [6] (RT article)

Facebook

Type	Private
Founded	Cambridge, Massachusetts (2004)
Founder	Mark Zuckerberg Chris Hughes Dustin Moskovitz Eduardo Saverin
Headquarters	Palo Alto, California, U.S. (main headquarters; serves the Americas) Dublin, Ireland (headquarters for Europe, Africa, Middle East) Seoul, South Korea (headquarters for Asia) Wellington, New Zealand (headquarters for Oceania), Hyderabad, India (Headquarters for South Asia)
Area served	Worldwide
Key people	Mark Zuckerberg (CEO) Chris Cox (VP of Product) Sheryl Sandberg (COO)
Revenue	▲ US$800 million (2009 est.)
Employees	1400 (2010)
Slogan		
Website	facebook.com [1]
Alexa rank	2 (August 2010)
Type of site	Social network service
Advertising	Banner ads, referral marketing, Casual games
Registration	Required
Users	500 million (active in July 2010)
Available in	Multilingual
Launched	February 4, 2004

Current status	Active

Facebook is a social network service and website launched in February 2004 that is operated and privately owned by Facebook, Inc. As of July 2010 Facebook has more than 500 million active users, which is about one person for every fourteen in the world. Users may create a personal profile, add other users as friends and exchange messages, including automatic notifications when they update their profile. Additionally, users may join common interest user groups, organized by workplace, school, or college, or other characteristics. The name of the service stems from the colloquial name of books given to students at the start of the academic year by university administrations in the US with the intention of helping students to get to know each other better. Facebook allows anyone who declares to be at least 13 years old to become a registered user of the website.

Facebook was founded by Mark Zuckerberg with his college roommates and fellow computer science students Eduardo Saverin, Dustin Moskovitz and Chris Hughes. The website's membership was initially limited by the founders to Harvard students, but was expanded to other colleges in the Boston area, the Ivy League, and Stanford University. It gradually added support for students at various other universities before opening to high school students, and, finally, to anyone aged 13 and over.

Facebook has met with some controversy. It has been blocked intermittently in several countries including Pakistan, Syria, the People's Republic of China, Vietnam,, Iran, and North Korea. It has also been banned at many places of work to discourage employees from wasting time using the service. Facebook's privacy has also been an issue, and the safety of their users has been compromised several times. Facebook settled a lawsuit regarding claims over source code and intellectual property. The site has also been involved in controversy over the sale of fans and friends.

A January 2009 Compete.com study ranked Facebook as the most used social network by worldwide monthly active users, followed by MySpace. *Entertainment Weekly* put it on its end-of-the-decade 'best-of' list, saying, "How on earth did we stalk our exes, remember our co-workers' birthdays, bug our friends, and play a rousing game of Scrabulous before Facebook?"

History

Main articles: History of Facebook and Timeline of Facebook

Mark Zuckerberg wrote Facemash, the predecessor to Facebook, on October 28, 2003, while attending Harvard as a sophomore. The site represented a Harvard University version of Hot or Not, according to the Harvard Crimson. According to *The Harvard Crimson*, Facemash "used photos compiled from the online facebooks of nine Houses, placing two next to each other at a time and asking users to choose the 'hotter' person."

Mark Zuckerberg co-created Facebook in his Harvard dorm room.

To accomplish this, Zuckerberg hacked into the protected areas of Harvard's computer network and copied the houses' private dormitory ID images. Harvard at that time did not have a student directory with photos and basic information, and the initial site generated 450 visitors and 22,000 photo-views in its first four hours online. That the initial site mirrored people's physical community—with their real identities—represented the key aspects of what later became Facebook.

The site was quickly forwarded to several campus group list-servers but was shut down a few days later by the Harvard administration. Zuckerberg was charged by the administration with breach of security, violating copyrights, and violating individual privacy, and faced expulsion, but ultimately the charges were dropped. Zuckerberg expanded on this initial project that semester by creating a social study tool ahead of an art history final by uploading 500 Augustan images to a website, with one image per page along with a comment section. He opened the site up to his classmates and people started sharing their notes.

The following semester, Zuckerberg began writing code for a new website in January 2004. He was inspired, he said, by an editorial in *The Harvard Crimson* about the Facemash incident. On February 4, 2004, Zuckerberg launched "Thefacebook", originally located at thefacebook.com.

Just six days after the site launched, three Harvard seniors, Cameron Winklevoss, Tyler Winklevoss, and Divya Narendra, accused Zuckerberg of intentionally misleading them into believing he would help them build a social network called HarvardConnection.com, while he was instead using their ideas to build a competing product. The three complained to the *Harvard Crimson* and the newspaper began an investigation. The three later filed a lawsuit against Zuckerberg, later settling.

Membership was initially restricted to students of Harvard College, and within the first month, more than half the undergraduate population at Harvard was registered on the service. Eduardo Saverin (business aspects), Dustin Moskovitz (programmer), Andrew McCollum (graphic artist), and Chris Hughes soon joined Zuckerberg to help promote the website. In March 2004, Facebook expanded to Stanford, Columbia, and Yale. This expansion continued when it opened to all Ivy League schools, Boston University, New York University, MIT, and gradually most universities in Canada and the United States.

Facebook incorporated in the summer of 2004 and the entrepreneur Sean Parker, who had been informally advising Zuckerberg, became the company's president. In June 2004, Facebook moved its base of operations to Palo Alto, California. Facebook received its first investment later that month from PayPal co-founder Peter Thiel. The company dropped *The* from its name after purchasing the domain name facebook.com in 2005 for $200,000.

Date	Users	Days later	Monthly growth
August 26, 2008	100	1665	178.38%
April 8, 2009	200	225	13.33%
September 15, 2009	300	150	10%
February 5, 2010	400	143	6.99%
July 21, 2010	500	166	4.52%
—	600	322 (ongoing)	

I+ Total active users (in millions) Facebook launched a high school version in September 2005, which Zuckerberg called the next logical step. At that time, high school networks required an invitation to join. Facebook later expanded membership eligibility to employees of several companies, including Apple Inc. and Microsoft. Facebook was then opened on September 26, 2006, to everyone of ages 13 and older with a valid e-mail address.

On October 24, 2007, Microsoft announced that it had purchased a 1.6% share of Facebook for $240 million, giving Facebook a total implied value of around $15 billion. Microsoft's purchase included rights to place international ads on Facebook. In October 2008, Facebook announced that it was to set up its international headquarters in Dublin, Ireland. In September 2009, Facebook claimed that it had turned cash flow positive for the first time. In June 2010, an online marketplace for trading private company stock reflected a valuation of $11.5 billion.

Traffic to Facebook has increased exponentially since 2009. More people visited Facebook than Google for the week ending March 13, 2010. Facebook has also become the top social network across eight individual markets in the region, Philippines, Australia, Indonesia, Malaysia, Singapore, New Zealand, Hong Kong and Vietnam, while other brands commanded the top positions in certain markets, including Google-owned Orkut in India, Mixi.jp in Japan, CyWorld in South Korea and Yahoo!'s Wretch.cc in Taiwan.[citation needed]

Company

Most of Facebook's revenues comes from advertising. Microsoft is Facebook's exclusive partner for serving banner advertising, and as such Facebook only serves advertisements that exist in Microsoft's advertisement inventory. According to comScore, an internet marketing research company, Facebook collects as much data from its visitors as Google and Microsoft, but considerably less than Yahoo!. In 2010, the security team began expanding its efforts to counter threats and terrorism from users. On November 6, 2007, Facebook launched Facebook Beacon, which was an ultimately failed attempt to advertise to friends of users using the knowledge of what purchases friends made.

Facebook generally has a lower clickthrough rate (CTR) for advertisements than most major websites. For banner advertisements, they have generally received one-fifth the number of clicks on Facebook compared to the Web as a whole. This means that a smaller percentage of Facebook's users click on advertisements than many other large websites. For example, while Google users click on the first advertisement for search results an average of 8% of the time (80,000 clicks for every one million searches), Facebook's users click on advertisements an average of 0.04% of the time (400 clicks for every one million pages).

Sarah Smith, who was Facebook's Online Sales Operations Manager, confirmed that successful advertising campaigns can have clickthrough rates as low as 0.05% to 0.04%, and that CTR for ads tend to fall within two weeks. Competing social network MySpace's CTR, in comparison, is about 0.1%, 2.5 times better than Facebook's but still low compared to many other websites. Explanations for Facebook's low CTR include the fact that Facebook's users are more technologically savvy and therefore use ad blocking software to hide advertisements, the users are younger and therefore are better at ignoring advertising messages, and that on MySpace, users spend more time browsing through content while on Facebook, users spend their time communicating with friends and therefore have their attention diverted away from advertisements.

Year	Revenue	Growth
2006	$52	—
2007	$150	188%
2008	$280	87%
2009	$800	186%
2010	$1100	38%

I+ Revenues

(estimated, in millions US$) On Pages for brands and products, however, some companies have reported CTR as high as 6.49% for Wall posts. Involver, a social marketing platform, announced in July 2008 that it managed to attain a CTR of 0.7% on Facebook (over 10 times the typical CTR for Facebook ad campaigns) for its first client, Serena Software, managing to convert 1.1 million views into 8000 visitors to their website. A study found that for video advertisements on Facebook, over 40% of users who viewed the videos viewed the entire video, while the industry average was 25% for in-banner video ads.

Facebook has approximately 1,400 employees and offices in eight countries. Regarding Facebook ownership, Mark Zuckerberg owns 24% of the company, Accel Partners owns 10%, Dustin Moskovitz owns 6%, Digital Sky Technologies owns 5%, Eduardo Saverin owns 5%, Sean Parker owns 4%, Peter Thiel owns 3%, Greylock Partners and Meritech Capital Partners own between 1 to 2% each, Microsoft owns 1.3%, Li Ka-shing owns 0.75%, the Interpublic Group owns less than 0.5%, a small group of current and former employees and celebrities own less than 1% each, including Matt Cohler, Jeff Rothschild, California U.S. Senator Barbara Boxer, Chris Hughes, and Owen Van Natta, while Reid Hoffman and Mark Pincus have sizable holdings of the company, and the remaining 30% or so are owned by employees, undisclosed number of celebrities, and outside investors. Adam D'Angelo, chief technology officer and friend of Zuckerberg, resigned in May 2008. Reports claimed that he and Zuckerberg began quarreling, and that he was no longer interested in partial ownership of the company.

Website

Main articles: Facebook features and Facebook Platform

Users can create profiles with photos, lists of personal interests, contact information and other personal information. Communicating with friends and other users can be done through private or public messages or a chat feature. Users can also create and join interest groups and "like pages" (formerly called "fan pages" until April 19, 2010), some of which are maintained by organizations as a means of advertising.

To allay concerns about privacy, Facebook enables users to choose their own privacy settings and choose who can see what parts of their profile. The website is free to users and generates revenue from advertising, such as banner ads. Facebook requires a user's name and profile picture (if applicable) to be accessible by everyone. Users can control who sees other information they have shared, as well as who can find them in searches, through their privacy settings.

The media often compares Facebook to MySpace, but one significant difference between the two websites is the level of customization. Another difference is Facebook's requirement that users utilize their true identity while MySpace does not. MySpace allows users to decorate their profiles using HTML and Cascading Style Sheets (CSS), while Facebook only allows plain text. Facebook has a number of features with which users may interact. They include the Wall, a space on every user's profile page that allows friends to post messages for the user to see;

Pokes, which allows users to send a virtual "poke" to each other (a notification then tells a user that they have been poked); Photos, where users can upload albums and photos; and Status, which allows users to inform their friends of their whereabouts and actions. Depending on privacy settings, anyone who can see a user's profile can also view that user's Wall. In July 2007, Facebook began allowing users to post attachments to the Wall, whereas the Wall was previously limited to textual content only.

Over time, Facebook has added features to its website. On September 6, 2006, a News Feed was announced, which appears on every user's homepage and highlights information including profile changes, upcoming events, and birthdays of the user's friends. This has enabled spammers and other users to manipulate these features by creating illegitimate events or posting fake birthdays to attract attention to their profile or cause. Initially, the News Feed caused dissatisfaction among Facebook users; some complained it was too cluttered and full of undesired information, while others were concerned it made it too easy for other people to track down individual activities (such as changes in relationship status, events, and conversations with other users).

In response to this dissatisfaction, Zuckerberg issued an apology for the site's failure to include appropriate customizable privacy features. Since then, users have been able to control what types of information are shared automatically with friends. Users are now able to prevent friends from seeing updates about certain types of activities, including profile changes, Wall posts, and newly added friends. On February 23, 2010, Facebook was granted US patent 7669123 [2] on certain aspects of their News Feed. The patent covers News Feeds where links are provided so that one user can participate in the same activity of another user. The patent may encourage Facebook to pursue action against websites that violate the patent, which may potentially include websites such as Twitter.

One of the most popular applications on Facebook is the Photos application, where users can upload albums and photos. Facebook allows users to upload an unlimited number of photos, compared with other image hosting services such as Photobucket and Flickr, which apply limits to the number of photos that a user is allowed to upload. During the first years, Facebook users were limited to 60 photos per album. As of May 2009, this limit has been increased to 200 photos per album.

Privacy settings can be set for individual albums, limiting the groups of users that can see an album. For example, the privacy of an album can be set so that only the user's friends can see the album, while the privacy of another album can be set so that all Facebook users can see it. Another feature of the Photos application is the ability to "tag", or label users in a photo. For instance, if a photo contains a user's friend, then the user can tag the friend in the photo. This sends a notification to the friend that they have been tagged, and provides them a link to see the photo.

Facebook Notes was introduced on August 22, 2006, a blogging feature that allowed tags and embeddable images. Users were later able to import blogs from Xanga, LiveJournal, Blogger, and other blogging services. During the week of April 7, 2008, Facebook released a Comet-based instant messaging application called "Chat" to several networks, which allows users to communicate with friends and is similar in functionality to desktop-based instant messengers.

Facebook launched Gifts on February 8, 2007, which allows users to send virtual gifts to their friends that appear on the recipient's profile. Gifts cost $1.00 each to purchase, and a personalized message can be attached to each gift. On May 14, 2007, Facebook launched Marketplace, which lets users post free classified ads. Marketplace has been compared to Craigslist by CNET, which points out that the major difference between the two is that listings posted by a user on Marketplace are only seen by users that are in the same network as that user, whereas listings posted on Craigslist can be seen by anyone.

On July 20, 2008, Facebook introduced "Facebook Beta", a significant redesign of its user interface on selected networks. The Mini-Feed and Wall were consolidated, profiles were separated into tabbed sections, and an effort was made to create a "cleaner" look. After initially giving users a choice to switch, Facebook began migrating all users to the new version beginning in September 2008. On

December 11, 2008, it was announced that Facebook was testing a simpler signup process.

On June 13, 2009, Facebook introduced a "Usernames" feature, whereby pages can be linked with simpler URLs such as http://www.facebook.com/facebook [3] as opposed to http://www.facebook.com/profile.php?id=20531316728 [4]. Many new smartphones offer access to the Facebook services either through their web-browsers or applications. An official Facebook application is available for the iPhone OS, the Android OS, and the WebOS. Nokia and Research in Motion both provide Facebook applications for their own mobile devices. More than 150 million active users access Facebook through mobile devices across 200 mobile operators in 60 countries.

Reception

See also: Criticism of Facebook

According to comScore, Facebook is the leading social networking site based on monthly unique visitors, having overtaken main competitor MySpace in April 2008. ComScore reports that Facebook attracted 130 million unique visitors in May 2010, an increase of 8.6 million people. According to Alexa, the website's ranking among all websites increased from 60th to 7th in worldwide traffic, from September 2006 to September 2007, and is currently 2nd. Quantcast ranks the website 2nd in the U.S. in traffic, and Compete.com ranks it 2nd in the U.S. The website is the most popular for uploading photos, with 50 billion uploaded cumulatively. In 2010, Sophos's "Security Threat Report 2010" polled over 500 firms, 60% of which responded that they believed that Facebook was the social network that posed the biggest threat to security, well ahead of MySpace, Twitter, and LinkedIn.

Facebook is the most popular social networking site in several English-speaking countries, including Canada, the United Kingdom, and the United States. In regional Internet markets, Facebook penetration is highest in North America (69 percent), Middle East-Africa (67 percent), Latin America (58 percent), Europe (57 percent), and Asia-Pacific (17 percent).

The website has won awards such as placement into the "Top 100 Classic Websites" by *PC Magazine* in 2007, and winning the "People's Voice Award" from the Webby Awards in 2008. In a 2006 study conducted by Student Monitor, a New Jersey-based company specializing in research concerning the college student market, Facebook was named the second most popular thing among undergraduates, tied with beer and only ranked lower than the iPod.

In 2010, Facebook won the Crunchie "Best Overall Startup Or Product" the third year in a row and was recognized as one of the "Hottest Silicon Valley Companies" by Lead411. However, in a July 2010 survey performed by the American Customer Satisfaction Index, Facebook received a score of 64 out of 100, placing it in the bottom 5% of all private sector companies in terms of customer satisfaction, alongside industries such as the IRS e-file system, airlines, and cable companies. Reasons for why Facebook scored so poorly include privacy problems, frequent changes to the website's interface, the results returned by the News Feed, and spam.

In December 2008, the Supreme Court of the Australian Capital Territory ruled that Facebook is a valid protocol to serve court notices to defendants. It is believed to be the world's first legal judgement that defines a summons posted on Facebook as legally binding. In March 2009, the New Zealand High Court associate justice David Glendall allowed for the serving of legal papers on Craig Axe by the company Axe Market Garden via Facebook. Employers (such as Virgin Atlantic Airways) have also used Facebook as a means to keep tabs on their employees and have even been known to fire them over posts they have made.

By 2005, the use of Facebook had already become so ubiquitous that the generic verb "facebooking" had come into use to describe the process of browsing others' profiles or updating one's own. In 2008, Collins English Dictionary declared "Facebook" as their new Word of the Year. In December 2009, the New Oxford American Dictionary declared their word of the year to be the verb "unfriend", defined as "To remove someone as a "friend" on a social networking site such as Facebook. As in, "I decided to unfriend my roommate on Facebook after we had a fight.""

As of April 2010, according to *The New York Times*, countries with most Facebook users are the United States, the United Kingdom and Indonesia. Also in early 2010, Openbook was established, an avowed parody website (and privacy advocacy website) that enables text-based searches of those Wall posts that are available to "Everyone," i.e. to everyone on the Internet.

Facebook has become a target for internet trolling where, when a person passes away and someone makes a memorial page for them, they would upload grotesque photos of mutilated bodies and poke fun at the deceased. Recently, a Delta, British Columbia teenager was attacked and killed, and the trolls pounced on the memorial page, disturbing friends and bringing grief to the family.

Impact

Facebook's effect on the American political system became clear in January 2008, shortly before the New Hampshire primary, when Facebook teamed up with ABC and Saint Anselm College to allow users to give live feedback about the "back to back" January 5 Republican and Democratic debates. Charles Gibson moderated both debates, held at the Dana Center for the Humanities at Saint Anselm College. Facebook users took part in debate groups organized around specific topics, register to vote, and message questions.

The stage at the Facebook – Saint Anselm College debates in 2008.

Over 1,000,000 people installed the Facebook application 'US politics' in order to take part, and the application measured users' responses to specific comments made by the debating candidates. This debate showed the broader community what many young students had already experienced: Facebook was an extremely popular and powerful new way to interact and voice opinions. An article written by Michelle Sullivan of Uwire.com illustrates how the "facebook effect" has affected youth voting rates, support by youth of political candidates, and general involvement by the youth population in the 2008 election.

In February 2008, a Facebook group called "One Million Voices Against FARC" organized an event that saw hundreds of thousands of Colombians march in protest against the Revolutionary Armed Forces of Colombia, better known as the FARC (from the group's Spanish name). In August 2010, one of North Korea's official government websites, Uriminzokkiri, joined Facebook.

In media

- At age 102, Ivy Bean of Bradford, England joined Facebook in 2008, making her one of the oldest people ever on Facebook. An inspiration to other residents, she quickly became more widely known and several fan pages were made in her honor. She visited Prime Minister Gordon Brown and his wife, Sarah, in Downing Street early in 2010. Some time after creating her Facebook page, Bean also joined Twitter, when she passed the maximum number of friends allowed by Facebook. She became the oldest person to ever use the Twitter website. At the time of her death in July 2010, she had 4,962 friends on Facebook and more than 56,000 followers on Twitter. Her death was widely reported in the media and she received tributes from several notable media personalities.
- "FriendFace", a December 2008 episode of the British sitcom, *The IT Crowd*, parodied Facebook and social networking sites, in general.
- American author, Ben Mezrich, published a book in July 2009 about Mark Zuckerberg and the founding of Facebook, titled *The Accidental Billionaires: The Founding of Facebook, A Tale of Sex, Money, Genius, and Betrayal*. In response to the Everybody Draw Mohammed Day controversy and the ban of the website in Pakistan, an Islamic version of the website was created, called MillatFacebook.
- "You Have 0 Friends", an April 2010 episode of the American animated comedy series, *South Park*, parodied Facebook.
- *The Social Network*, a comedy-drama film directed by David Fincher about the founding of Facebook, was released October 1, 2010. The film features an ensemble cast consisting of Jesse Eisenberg as Mark Zuckerberg, Justin Timberlake as Sean Parker, Brenda Song as Christy Lee, Andrew Garfield as Eduardo Saverin, Rooney Mara as Erica, and Armie Hammer as Cameron and Tyler Winklevoss. The film was written by Aaron Sorkin and adapted from Ben Mezrich's 2009 book. The film is being distributed by Columbia Pictures. None of the Facebook staff, including Zuckerberg, is involved with the project. However, one of Facebook's co-founders, Eduardo Saverin, was a consultant for Mezrich's book.

See also

- Ambient Awareness
- CampusNetwork
- Diaspora (software)
- *The Facebook Era* (book)
- List of social networking websites
- Social Media
- Wirehog

External links

- Official website [1]
- "Facebook news and reviews" [5] at *The Daily Telegraph*
- ☷ The Wiktionary definition of facebook
- ☙ Media related to Facebook at Wikimedia Commons

ckb:فۆیسبووک

Advertise Yourself

AdWords

Google AdWords	
Developer(s)	Google Inc.
Initial release	October 23, 2000
Operating system	Cross-platform (web-based application)
Type	Online advertising
Website	www.google.com/adwords [1]

AdWords is Google's flagship advertising product and main source of revenue. Google's total advertising revenues were USD$23 billion in 2009. AdWords offers pay-per-click (PPC) advertising, and site-targeted advertising for both text, banner, and rich-media ads. The AdWords program includes local, national, and international distribution. Google's text advertisements are short, consisting of one headline and two additional text lines. Image ads can be one of several different Interactive Advertising Bureau (IAB) standard sizes.

Sales and Support for Google's AdWords division is based in Mountain View, California, with major secondary offices in Ann Arbor, Michigan, the company's third-largest US facility behind its Mountain View, California, headquarters and New York City office. Engineering for AdWords is based in Mountain View, California.

Pay-Per-Click advertisements (PPC)

Advertisers select the words that should trigger their ads and the maximum amount they will pay per click. When a user searches Google's search engine on www.google.com or the relevant local/national google server (e.g. www.google.co.uk for The United Kingdom), ads (also known as creatives by Google) for relevant words are shown as "sponsored links" on the right side of the screen, and sometimes above the main search results. Clickthrough rates (CTR) for the ads are about 8% for the first ad, 5% for the second one, and 2.5% for the third one. Search results can return from 0 to 12 ads.

The ordering of the paid-for listings depends on other advertisers' bids (PPC) and the "quality score" of all ads shown for a given search. The quality score is calculated by historical click-through rates, relevance of an advertiser's ad text and keywords, an advertiser's account history, and other relevance factors as determined by Google. The quality score is also used by Google to set the minimum bids for an advertiser's keywords. The minimum bid takes into consideration the quality of the landing page as well, which includes the relevancy and originality of content, navigability, and transparency into the nature of the business. Though Google has released a list of full guidelines for sites, the precise formula and meaning of relevance and its definition is in part secret to Google and the parameters used can change dynamically.

The auction mechanism that determines the order of the ads is a generalized second-price auction. This is claimed to have the property that the participants *do not necessarily* fare best when they truthfully reveal any private information asked for by the auction mechanism (in this case, the value of the keyword to them, in the form of a "truthful" bid).

AdWords Features

IP Address Exclusion

> In addition to controlling ad placements through methods such as location and language targeting, ad targeting can be refined with Internet Protocol (IP) address exclusion. This feature enables advertisers to specify IP address ranges where they don't want their ads to appear.

> Up to 20 IP addresses, or ranges of addresses, can be excluded per campaign. All ads in the campaign are prevented from showing for users with the IP addresses specified.

> Location-based exclusion is also offered as a method of narrowing targeted users.

Frequency Capping

> Frequency capping limits the number of times ads appear to the same unique user on the Google Content Network. It doesn't apply to the Search Network. If frequency capping is enabled for a campaign, a limit must be specified as to the number of impressions allowed per day, week, or month for an individual user. The cap can be configured to apply to each ad, ad group, or campaign.

Placement targeted advertisements (formerly Site-Targeted Advertisements)

In 2003 Google introduced site-targeted advertising. Using the AdWords control panel, advertisers can enter keywords, domain names, topics, and demographic targeting preferences, and Google places the ads on what they see as relevant sites within their content network. If domain names are targeted, Google also provides a list of related sites for placement. Advertisers may bid on a cost per impression (CPM) or cost per click (CPC) basis for site targeting.

With placement targeting, it is possible for an ad to take up the entire ad block rather than have the ad block split into 2 to 4 ads, resulting in higher visibility for the advertiser.

The minimum cost-per-thousand impressions bid for placement targeted campaigns is 25 cents. There is no minimum CPC bid, however.

AdWords distribution

All AdWords ads are eligible to be shown on www.google.com. Advertisers also have the option of enabling their ads to show on Google's partner networks. The "search network" includes AOL search, Ask.com, and Netscape. Like www.google.com, these search engines show AdWords ads in response to user searches, but do not effect quality score.

The "Google Display Network" (formerly referred to as the "content network") shows AdWords ads on sites that are not search engines. These content network sites are those that use AdSense and DoubleClick, the other side of the Google advertising model. AdSense is used by website owners who wish to make money by displaying ads on their websites. Click through rates on the display network are typically much lower than those on the search network and are therefore ignored when calculating an advertiser's quality score. It has been reported that using both AdSense and AdWords may cause a website to pay Google a commission when the website advertises itself.

Google automatically determines the subject of pages and displays relevant ads based on the advertisers' keyword lists. AdSense publishers may select channels to help direct Google's ad placements on their pages, to increase performance of their ad units. There are many different types of ads that can run across Google's network, including text ads, image ads (banner ads), mobile text ads, and in-page video ads.

Google AdWords' main competitors are Yahoo! Search Marketing and Microsoft adCenter.

AdWords account management

To help clients with the complexity of building and managing AdWords accounts search engine marketing agencies and consultants offer account management as a business service. This has allowed organizations without advertising expertise to reach a global, online audience. Google has started the Google Advertising Professionals program to certify agencies and consultants who have met specific qualifications and passed an exam. Google also provides account management software, called AdWords Editor [2].

Another useful feature is the My Client Centre available to Google Professionals (even if not yet passed the exam or budget parameters) whereby a Google professional has access and a dashboard summary of several accounts and can move between those accounts without logging in to each account.

The Google Adwords Keyword Tool provides a list of related keywords for a specific website or keyword.

Recently, numerous complaints have been filed with the San Jose Better Business Bureau (BBB) regarding treatment small businesses have received from Google Adwords customer service. As a result, the company now has a C- rating with the San Jose BBB.

Click-to-Call

Google Click-to-Call was a service provided by Google which allows users to call advertisers from Google search results pages. Users enter their phone number, Google calls them back and connects to the advertiser. Calling charges are paid by Google. It was discontinued in 2007.. For some time similar click-to-call functionality was available for results in Google Maps. In the Froyo release of Google's operating system, in certain advertisements, there is a very similar functionality, where a user can easily call an advertiser.

History

The original idea was invented by Bill Gross from Idealab who, in turn borrowed the idea from Yellow Pages. Google wanted to buy the idea but a deal could not be reached.[citation needed] Not wanting to give up on this form of advertisement, the company launched its own solution, AdWords in 2000.. AdWords followed a model that was significantly similar to Bill Gross' creation which led to legal action between the two parties. Eventually the dispute was settled out of court.[citation needed]

At first AdWords advertisers would pay a monthly amount, and Google would then set up and manage their campaign. To accommodate small businesses and those who wanted to manage their own campaigns, Google soon introduced the AdWords self-service portal. Starting in 2005 Google provided a campaign management service called Jumpstart to assist advertisers in setting up their campaigns. However, this service is no longer available, so companies needing assistance must hire a third-party service provider.

In 2005, Google launched the Google Advertising Professional (GAP) Program to certify individuals and companies who completed AdWords training and passed an exam. Due to the complexity of AdWords and the amount of money at stake, some advertisers hire a consultant to manage their campaigns.

In 2008, Google launched the Google Online Marketing Challenge (http:// www. google. com/ onlinechallenge/), an in-class academic exercise for tertiary students. Over 8,000 students from 47 countries participated in the 2008 Challenge and over 10,000 students from 58 countries took part in 2009. The Challenge runs annually, roughly from January to June. Registration [3] is at the instructor rather than student level.

In 2009, Google revised the AdWords interface, introduced Local Business Ads for Google Maps and Video Ads.

Legal context

AdWords has generated lawsuits in the area of trademark law (see Google, Inc. v. Am. Blind & Wallpaper Factory and Rescuecom Corp. v. Google, Inc.), fraud (see Goddard v. Google, Inc.), and click fraud. In 2006, Google settled a click fraud lawsuit for US$90 million.

Overture Services, Inc. sued Google for patent infringement in April 2002 in relation to the AdWords service. Following Yahoo!'s acquisition of Overture, the suit was settled in 2004 with Google agreeing to issue 2.7 million shares of common stock to Yahoo! in exchange for a perpetual license under the patent.

Technology

The AdWords system was initially implemented on top of the MySQL database engine. After the system had been launched, management decided to use a commercial database (Oracle) instead. The system became much slower, so eventually it was returned to MySQL [4]. The interface has also been revamped to offer better work flow with additional new features, such as Spreadsheet Editing, Search Query Reports, and better conversion metrics.

As of April 2008 Google AdWords no longer allows for the display URL to deviate from that of the destination URL. Prior to its introduction, Google paid advertisements could feature different landing page URLs to that of what was being displayed on the search network. Google expounds that the policy change stems from both user and advertiser feedback. The concern prompting the restriction change is believed to be the premise on which users clicked advertisements. Users were in some cases, being misled and further targeted by AdWords advertisers.

Google has other restrictions, for example the advertising of a book by Aaron Greenspan called *Authoritas: One Student's Harvard Admissions and the Founding of the Facebook Era*, was restricted from advertising on AdWords because it contained the word Facebook in it. Google's rationale was that it was prohibited from advertising a book which used a trademarked name in its title.

Allowed keywords

Google has also come under fire for allowing AdWords advertisers to bid on trademarked keywords. In 2004, Google started allowing advertisers to bid on a wide variety of search terms in the US and Canada, including the trademarks of their competitors and in May 2008 expanded this policy to the UK and Ireland. Advertisers are restricted from using other companies' trademarks in their advertisement text if the trademark has been registered with Advertising Legal Support team. Google does, however, require certification to run regulated keywords, such as those related to pharmaceuticals keywords, and some keywords, such as those related to hacking, are not allowed at all. These restrictions may vary by location. From June 2007, Google banned AdWords adverts for student essay writing services, a move which was welcomed by universities.

See also

- AdSense
- List of Google tools and services
- Click fraud
- Search engine marketing
- Central ad server
- Performance-based advertising
- Search analytics

External links

- Google AdWords [5]
- Google AdWords: Keyword Tool [6]

Upload a Video Resume

Video resume

A **video resume** is a way for job seekers to showcase their abilities beyond the capabilities of a traditional paper resume. The video resume allows prospective employers to see, hear and get a feel for how the applicant presents themselves.

History

Video resumes (or Video CV in UK terminology) were first introduced in the 1980s for use and distribution via VHS tape, but the idea never took off beyond the video taping of interviews. However, with the modern capabilities of transmitting streaming video via the internet, video resumes have taken on new popularity. Video resumes are now being widely accepted by companies throughout the world for varying professions and the need for objectivity in these videos is becoming a serious issue.[citation needed] Many copycat video resume companies have sites where people can upload their own videos, but companies are shying away from accepting homemade, webcam pieces.[citation needed]

Criticism

With the popularity of video hosting solutions there has been much debate in the usefulness of video resumes. Most recruiters feel that a video alone does not give an employer enough information about a candidate to make a proper evaluation of the applicant's potential and more importantly skills. One article suggests that

> "While a video resume introduces applicants on camera, the value such visual imagery adds is debatable. A text resume allows for specific pieces of information to be parsed out and compared across candidates. When the information is delivered verbally, recruiters need to glean the details themselves."

Video resumes can serve to facilitate racial, ethnic, class-based and age discrimination, or lead to accusations of such discrimination.

New trends

With the rise in video-hosting sites like YouTube and broadband Internet usage, video résumés are becoming more popular. Several sites have been created for video resume hosting. Support for video resumes is growing[citation needed] as more complete solutions evolve.

There are other websites however who do not shy away hosting immature home made video resumes besides professinally built video resumes. One such resume hosting site that freely caters each type of video resume is www.recruittube.com [1] . There are many types of synonyms to video resume are being seen now a day they include visual resume, visual CV, Animated Resume, Animated CV, Resume Reel, Visual portfolio and self-introduction etc.

External links

- Stephen J. Dubner, author of *Freakonomics* on video resumes [2]
- Job seekers show rather than tell [3] article from *USA Today*
- Video Resumes: Lights, Camera, Hire Me [4] article from *ABC News*

YouTube

Type	Subsidiary, limited liability company
Founded	February 2005
Founder	Steve Chen, Chad Hurley, Jawed Karim
Headquarters	901 Cherry Ave, San Bruno, California, United States
Area served	Worldwide
Key people	Chad Hurley (CEO) Steve Chen (CTO) Jawed Karim (Advisor)
Owner	YouTube LLC (2005–2006) Google Inc. (2006–present)
Slogan	Broadcast Yourself
Website	YouTube.com [1] (see list of localized domain names)
Alexa rank	3 (July 2010)
Type of site	video hosting service
Advertising	Google AdSense
Registration	Optional
Available in	29 languages are available through the user interface
Launched	February 14, 2005
Current status	Active

YouTube is a video-sharing website on which users can upload, share, and view videos. Three former PayPal employees created YouTube in February 2005.

The company is based in San Bruno, California, and uses Adobe Flash Video technology to display a wide variety of user-generated video content, including movie clips, TV clips, and music videos, as well as amateur content such as video blogging and short original videos. Most of the content on YouTube has been uploaded by individuals, although media corporations including CBS, BBC, VEVO and other organizations offer some of their material via the site, as part of the YouTube partnership program.

Unregistered users can watch the videos, while registered users are permitted to upload an unlimited number of videos. Videos that are considered to contain potentially offensive content are available only to registered users 18 and older. In November 2006, YouTube, LLC was bought by Google Inc. for $1.65 billion, and now operates as a subsidiary of Google.

Company history

Main article: History of YouTube

YouTube's current headquarters in San Bruno, California

YouTube was founded by Chad Hurley, Steve Chen and Jawed Karim, who were all early employees of PayPal. Hurley studied design at Indiana University of Pennsylvania, while Chen and Karim studied computer science together at the University of Illinois at Urbana-Champaign.

According to a story that has often been repeated in the media, Chad Hurley and Steve Chen developed the idea for YouTube during the early months of 2005, after they had experienced difficulty sharing videos that had been shot at a dinner party at Chen's apartment in San Francisco. Jawed Karim did not attend the party and denied that it had occurred, while Chad Hurley commented that the idea that YouTube was founded after a dinner party "was probably very strengthened by marketing ideas around creating a story that was very digestible."

YouTube began as a venture-funded technology startup, primarily from a US$11.5 million investment by Sequoia Capital between November 2005 and April 2006. YouTube's early headquarters were situated above a pizzeria and Japanese restaurant in San Mateo, California. The domain name www.youtube.com was activated on February 14, 2005, and the website was developed over the subsequent months. The first YouTube video was entitled *Me at the zoo*, and shows founder Jawed Karim at San Diego Zoo. The video was uploaded on April 23, 2005, and can still be viewed on the site.

YouTube offered the public a beta test of the site in May 2005, six months before the official launch in November 2005. The site grew rapidly, and in July 2006 the company announced that more than 65,000 new videos were being uploaded every day, and that the site was receiving 100 million video views per day. According to data published by market research company comScore, YouTube is the dominant provider of online video in the United States, with a market share of around 43 percent and more than 14 billion videos viewed in May 2010. YouTube says that 24 hours of new videos are uploaded to the site every minute, and that around three quarters of the material comes from outside the United States. It is estimated that in 2007 YouTube consumed as much bandwidth as the entire Internet in 2000. Alexa ranks YouTube as the third most visited website on the Internet, behind Google and

Facebook.

The choice of the name www.youtube.com led to problems for a similarly named website, www.utube.com. The owner of the site, Universal Tube & Rollform Equipment, filed a lawsuit against YouTube in November 2006 after being overloaded on a regular basis by people looking for YouTube. Universal Tube has since changed the name of its website to www.utubeonline.com. In October 2006, Google Inc. announced that it had acquired YouTube for US$1.65 billion in Google stock, and the deal was finalized on November 13, 2006. Google does not provide detailed figures for YouTube's running costs, and YouTube's revenues in 2007 were noted as "not material" in a regulatory filing. In June 2008, a Forbes magazine article projected the 2008 revenue at US$200 million, noting progress in advertising sales.

In November 2008, YouTube reached an agreement with MGM, Lions Gate Entertainment and CBS, allowing the companies to post full-length films and television episodes on the site, accompanied by advertisements in a section for US viewers called "Shows". The move was intended to create competition with websites such as Hulu, which features material from NBC, Fox, and Disney. In November 2009, YouTube launched a version of "Shows" available to UK viewers, offering around 4000 full-length shows from more than 60 partners. In January 2010, YouTube introduced an online film rentals service, which is currently available only to users in the United States.

In March 2010, YouTube began free streaming of certain content, including 60 cricket matches of the Indian Premier League. According to YouTube, this was the first worldwide free online broadcast of a major sporting event.

On March 31, 2010, the YouTube website launched a new design, with the aim of simplifying the interface and increasing the time users spend on the site. Google product manager Shiva Rajaraman commented: "We really felt like we needed to step back and remove the clutter." In May 2010, it was reported that YouTube was serving more than two billion videos a day, which it described as "nearly double the prime-time audience of all three major US television networks combined."

Social impact

Main article: Social impact of YouTube

Before the launch of YouTube in 2005, there were few easy methods available for ordinary computer users who wanted to post videos online. With its simple interface, YouTube made it possible for anyone with an Internet connection to post a video that a worldwide audience could watch within a few minutes. The wide range of topics covered by YouTube has turned video sharing into one of the most important parts of Internet culture.

An early example of the social impact of YouTube was the success of the Bus Uncle video in 2006. It shows a heated conversation between a youth and an older man on a bus in Hong Kong, and was discussed widely in the mainstream media. Another YouTube video to receive extensive coverage is *guitar*, which features a performance of Pachelbel's Canon on an electric guitar. The name of the performer is not given in the video, and after it received millions of views *The New York Times* revealed the identity of the guitarist as Jeong-Hyun Lim, a 23-year-old from South Korea who had recorded the track in his bedroom.

YouTube was awarded a 2008 George Foster Peabody Award and cited for being "a 'Speakers' Corner' that both embodies and promotes democracy." *Entertainment Weekly* put it on its end-of-the-decade, "best-of" list, saying, "Providing a safe home for piano-playing cats, celeb goof-ups, and overzealous lip-synchers since 2005."

Criticism

Main article: Criticism of YouTube

Copyrighted material

YouTube has been criticized for failing to ensure that uploaded videos comply with the law of copyright. At the time of uploading a video, YouTube users are shown a screen with the message "Do not upload any TV shows, music videos, music concerts or advertisements without permission, unless they consist entirely of content that you created yourself". Despite this advice, there are still many unauthorized clips of copyrighted material on YouTube. YouTube does not view videos before they are posted online, and it is left to copyright holders to issue a takedown notice under the terms of the Digital Millennium Copyright Act.

Organizations including Viacom, Mediaset and the English Premier League have filed lawsuits against YouTube, claiming that it has done too little to prevent the uploading of copyrighted material. Viacom, demanding US$1 billion in damages, said that it had found more than 150,000 unauthorized clips of its material on YouTube that had been viewed "an astounding 1.5 billion times". YouTube responded by stating that it "goes far beyond its legal obligations in assisting content owners to protect their works". Since Viacom filed its lawsuit, YouTube has introduced a system called Video ID, which checks uploaded videos against a database of copyrighted content with the aim of reducing violations. On June 23, 2010, Viacom's lawsuit against Google was rejected in a summary judgment, with Judge Louis Stanton stating that Google was protected by provisions of the Digital Millennium Copyright Act. Viacom announced its intention to appeal against the ruling.

In August 2008, a U.S. court ruled in Lenz v. Universal Music Corp. that copyright holders cannot order the removal of an online file without first determining whether the posting reflected fair use of the material. The case involved Stephanie Lenz from Gallitzin, Pennsylvania, who had made a home video of her 13-month-old son dancing to Prince's song "Let's Go Crazy" and posted the 29-second video on YouTube.

Privacy

In July 2008, Viacom won a court ruling requiring YouTube to hand over data detailing the viewing habits of every user who has watched videos on the site. The move led to concerns that the viewing habits of individual users could be identified through a combination of their IP addresses and login names. The decision was criticized by the Electronic Frontier Foundation, which called the court ruling "a set-back to privacy rights". U.S. District Court Judge Louis Stanton dismissed the privacy concerns as "speculative", and ordered YouTube to hand over documents totalling around 12 terabytes of data. Judge Stanton rejected Viacom's request for YouTube to hand over the source code of its search engine system, saying that there was no evidence that YouTube treated videos infringing copyright differently.

Controversial content

YouTube has also faced criticism over the offensive content in some of its videos. The uploading of videos containing defamation, pornography and material encouraging criminal conduct is prohibited by YouTube's terms of service. Controversial areas for videos have included conspiracy theories, religion, Holocaust denial, and the Hillsborough Disaster, in which 96 football fans from Liverpool were crushed to death in 1989.

YouTube relies on its users to flag the content of videos as inappropriate, and a YouTube employee will view a flagged video to determine whether it violates the site's terms of service. However, this procedure has been criticized by the United Kingdom government: in July 2008 the Culture and Media Committee of the House of Commons of the United Kingdom stated that it was "unimpressed" with YouTube's system for policing its videos, and argued that "Proactive review of content should be standard practice for sites hosting user generated content." YouTube responded by stating: "We have strict rules on what's allowed, and a system that enables anyone who sees inappropriate content to report it to our 24/7 review team and have it dealt with promptly. We educate our community on the rules and include a direct link from every YouTube page to make this process as easy as possible for our users. Given the volume of content uploaded on our site, we think this is by far the most effective way to make sure that the tiny minority of videos that break the rules come down quickly."

Blocking

Main article: Censorship of YouTube

Several countries have blocked access to YouTube:

- The People's Republic of China blocked YouTube to prevent dissemination of July 2009 Ürümqi riots video.
- Morocco shut down access to YouTube in 2008.
- Thailand blocked YouTube between 2006 and 2007 due to offensive videos relating to King Bhumibol Adulyadej.

- YouTube is currently blocked in Turkey after controversy over videos deemed insulting to Mustafa Kemal Atatürk. Despite the block, Prime Minister of Turkey Recep Tayyip Erdoğan admitted to journalists that he could access YouTube, since the site is still available in Turkey by using an open proxy.
- On December 3, 2006, Iran temporarily blocked access to YouTube, along with several other sites, after declaring them as violating social and moral codes of conduct. The YouTube block came after a video was posted online that appeared to show an Iranian soap opera star having sex. The block was later lifted and then reinstated after Iran's 2009 presidential election.
- On February 23, 2008, Pakistan blocked YouTube because of "offensive material" towards the Islamic faith, including display of the Danish cartoons of the prophet Muhammad. This led to a near global blackout of the YouTube site for around two hours, as the Pakistani block was inadvertently transferred to other countries. Pakistan lifted its block on February 26, 2008. Many Pakistanis circumvented the three-day block by using virtual private network software. In May 2010, following the Everybody Draw Mohammed Day, Pakistan again blocked access to YouTube, citing "growing sacrilegious content".
- On January 24, 2010, Libya blocked access to YouTube after it featured videos of demonstrations in the Libyan city of Benghazi by families of detainees who were killed in Abu Salim prison in 1996, and videos of family members of Libyan leader Moamer Kadhafi at parties. The blocking was criticized by Human Rights Watch.

Some schools have blocked access to YouTube, citing the inability to determine what sort of video material might be accessed by students.

Features

Main article: Features of YouTube

Video technology

Playback

Viewing YouTube videos on a personal computer requires the Adobe Flash Player plug-in to be installed in the browser. The Adobe Flash Player plug-in is one of the most common pieces of software installed on personal computers and accounts for almost 75% of online video material.

In January 2010, YouTube launched an experimental version of the site that uses the built-in multimedia capabilities of web browsers supporting the HTML5 standard. This allows videos to be viewed without requiring Adobe Flash Player or any other plug-in to be installed. The YouTube site has a page that allows supported browsers to opt in to the HTML5 trial. Only browsers that support HTML5 Video using the H.264 or WebM formats can play the videos, and not all videos on the site are available.

Uploading

Videos uploaded to YouTube by standard account holders are limited to 15 minutes in duration. When YouTube was launched in 2005 it was possible to upload longer videos, but a ten minute limit was introduced in March 2006 after YouTube found that the majority of videos exceeding this length were unauthorized uploads of television shows and films. The ten minute limit was increased to fifteen minutes in July 2010. Partner accounts are permitted to upload longer videos, subject to acceptance by YouTube. File size is limited to 2 GB for uploads from YouTube web page, and to 20 GB if Java-based Advanced Uploader is used.

YouTube accepts videos uploaded in most container formats, including .AVI, .MKV, .MOV, .MP4, DivX, .FLV, and .ogg and .ogv. These include video formats such as MPEG-4, MPEG, and .WMV. It also supports 3GP, allowing videos to be uploaded from legacy mobile phones. Videos with progressive scanning or interlaced scanning can be uploaded, but for the best video quality, YouTube prefers interlaced videos to be deinterlaced prior to uploading. All the video formats on YouTube use progressive scanning.

Quality and codecs

YouTube originally offered videos at only one quality level, displayed at a resolution of 320x240 pixels using the H.263 Sorenson Spark codec, with mono MP3 audio. In June 2007, YouTube added an option to watch videos in 3GP format on mobile phones. In March 2008, a high quality mode was added, which increased the resolution to 480x360 pixels In November 2008 720p HD support was added. With this new feature, YouTube began a switchover to H.264/MPEG-4 AVC as its default video codec. In November 2008, the YouTube player was also changed from a 4:3 aspect ratio to a widescreen 16:9. In November 2009, 1080p HD support was added. In July 2010, YouTube announced that it had launched a range of videos in 4k format, which allows a resolution of up to 4096x3072 pixels.

YouTube videos are available in a range of quality levels. The former names of standard quality (SQ), high quality (HQ) and high definition (HD) have been replaced by numerical values representing the vertical resolution of the video. The default video stream is encoded in H.264/MPEG-4 AVC format, with stereo AAC audio.

Comparison of YouTube media encoding options

fmt value[1]	5	34	35	18	22	37	38	43	45	17
Default container	FLV			MP4				WebM		3GP

		H.263	MPEG-4 AVC (H.264)						VP8		MPEG-4 Visual
Video	**Encoding**	H.263	MPEG-4 AVC (H.264)						VP8		MPEG-4 Visual
	Max width (pixels)	400	640	854	480	1280	1920	4096	854	1280	176
	Max height (pixels)	240	360	480	360	720	1080	3072	480	720	144
	Bitrate[2] (Mbit/s)	0.25	0.5	0.8 - 1	0.5	2	3.5 - 5	–	–	–	–
Audio	**Encoding**	MP3	AAC						Vorbis		AAC
	Channels	1–2	2 (stereo)								
	Sampling rate (Hz)	22050	44100					48000	44100		
	Bitrate, Kbit/s[2]	–	–	–	–	–	–	–	96	128	–

1 *fmt* is an undocumented URL parameter that allows selecting YouTube quality mode without using player user interface.

2 Approximate values based on statistical data; actual bitrate can be higher or lower due to variable encoding rate.

3D videos

In a video posted on July 21, 2009, YouTube software engineer Peter Bradshaw announced that YouTube users can now upload 3D videos. The videos can be viewed in several different ways, including the common anaglyph (cyan/red lens) method which utilizes glasses worn by the viewer to achieve the 3D effect.

Content accessibility

One of the key features of YouTube is the ability of users to view its videos on web pages outside the site. Each YouTube video is accompanied by a piece of HTML, which can be used to embed it on a page outside the YouTube website. This functionality is often used to embed YouTube videos in social networking pages and blogs. Embedding, as well as ranking and commenting, can be disabled by the video owner.

YouTube does not usually offer a download link for its videos, and intends that they are viewed through its website interface. A small number of videos, such as the weekly addresses by President Barack Obama, can be downloaded as MP4 files. Numerous third-party web sites, applications and browser plug-ins allow users to download YouTube videos. In February 2009, YouTube announced a test service, allowing some partners to offer video downloads for free or for a fee paid through Google Checkout.

Platforms

Some smart phones are capable of accessing YouTube videos, dependent on the provider and the data plan. YouTube Mobile was launched in June 2007, and uses RTSP streaming for the video. Not all of YouTube's videos are available on the mobile version of the site.

Since June 2007, YouTube's videos have been available for viewing on a range of Apple products. This required YouTube's content to be transcoded into Apple's preferred video standard, H.264, a process that took several months. YouTube videos can be viewed on devices including Apple TV, iPod Touch and the iPhone. A TiVo service update in July 2008 allowed the system to search and play YouTube videos. In January 2009, YouTube launched "YouTube for TV", a version of the website tailored for set-top boxes and other TV-based media devices with web browsers, initially allowing its videos to be viewed on the PlayStation 3 and Wii video game consoles. In June 2009, YouTube XL was introduced, which has a simplified interface designed for viewing on a standard television screen.

Localization

On June 19, 2007, Google CEO Eric E. Schmidt was in Paris to launch the new localization system. The interface of the website is available with localized versions in 24 countries and a worldwide version.

Country	Language	Launch date
Argentina	Spanish	September 8, 2010
Australia	English (Australia)	October 22, 2007
Brazil	Portuguese (Brazil)	June 19, 2007
Canada	English (Canada) and French (Canada)	November 6, 2007
Czech Republic	Czech	October 9, 2008
France	French	June 19, 2007
Germany	German	November 8, 2007
Hong Kong	English and Chinese (Traditional)	October 17, 2007
Israel	Hebrew	September 16, 2008
India	English (India) and Hindi	May 7, 2008
Ireland	English (Ireland)	June 19, 2007
Italy	Italian	June 19, 2007
Japan	Japanese	June 19, 2007

Korea	Korean	January 23, 2008
Mexico	Spanish (Mexico)	October 11, 2007
Netherlands	Dutch	June 19, 2007
New Zealand	English (New Zealand)	October 22, 2007
Poland	Polish	June 19, 2007
Russia	Russian	November 13, 2007
Spain	Spanish	June 19, 2007
South Africa	English (South African)	May 17, 2010
Sweden	Swedish	October 22, 2008
Taiwan	Chinese (Traditional)	October 18, 2007
United Kingdom	English (United Kingdom)	June 19, 2007

The YouTube interface suggests which local version should be chosen on the basis of the IP address of the user. In some cases, the message "This video is not available in your country" may appear because of copyright restrictions or inappropriate content.

The interface of the YouTube website is available in 29 different languages, including Danish, Finnish, Greek, Hungarian, Slovenian and Norwegian, which do not have local channel versions.

Plans for YouTube to create a local version in Turkey have run into problems, since the Turkish authorities asked YouTube to set up an office in Turkey, which would be subject to Turkish law. YouTube says that it has no intention of doing this, and that its videos are not subject to Turkish law. Turkish authorities have expressed concerns that YouTube has been used to post videos insulting to Mustafa Kemal Atatürk and some material offensive to Muslims.

In March 2009, a dispute between YouTube and the British royalty collection agency PRS for Music led to premium music videos being blocked for YouTube users in the United Kingdom. The removal of videos posted by the major record companies occurred after failure to reach agreement on a licensing deal. The dispute was resolved in September 2009. In April 2009, a similar dispute led to the removal of premium music videos for users in Germany.

April Fools

YouTube has featured April Fools on the site every year since 2008:

- **2008:** All the links to the videos on the main page were redirected to Rick Astley's music video "Never Gonna Give You Up", a prank known as "Rickrolling".
- **2009:** When clicking on a video on the main page, the whole page turned upside down. YouTube claimed that this was a new layout.
- **2010:** YouTube temporarily released a "TEXTp" mode, which translated the colors in the videos to random upper case letters. YouTube claimed in a message that this was done in order to reduce bandwidth costs by $1 per second.

See also

- Alternative media
- CNN-YouTube presidential debates
- Comparison of video services
- List of Internet phenomena
- List of YouTube personalities
- Motion picture rating system#YouTube YouTube ratings
- Viral video
- YouTube Awards
- YouTube Live
- YouTube Instant

References

Bibliography

- Lacy, Sarah (2008). *The Stories of Facebook, YouTube and MySpace: The People, the Hype and the Deals Behind the Giants of Web 2.0.* Richmond: Crimson. ISBN 9781854584533

External links

- Official website [1]

pnb:بوی⌷ وی

Traditional Methods

Employment agency

An **employment agency** is an organization which matches employers to employees. In all developed countries there is a publicly funded employment agency and multiple private businesses which also act as employment agencies.

Public employment agencies

Since the beginning of the twentieth century, every developed country has created a public employment agency as a way to combat unemployment and help people find work.

In the United Kingdom the first agency began in London, through the Labour Bureau (London) Act 1902, and subsequently nationwide by the Labour/Liberal government through the Labour Exchanges Act 1909. The present public provider of job search help is called Jobcentre plus.

In the United States, a federal programme of employment services was rolled out in the New Deal. The initial legislation was called the Wagner-Peyser Act of 1933 and more recently job services happen through one-stop centres established by the Workforce Investment Act of 1998.

Private employment agencies

The first private employment agency in the United States was opened by Fred Winslow who opened Engineering Agency in 1893.[citation needed] It later became part of General Employment Enterprises who also owned Businessmen's Clearing House (est. 1902). Another of the oldest agencies was developed by Katharine Felton as a response to the problems brought on by the 1906 San Francisco earthquake and fire.

Many temporary agencies specialize in a particular profession or field of business, such as accounting, health care, technical, or secretarial.

Legal status

For most of the twentieth century, private employment agencies were considered quasi illegal entities under international law. The International Labour Organization instead called for the establishment of public employment agencies. To prevent the abusive practices of private agencies, they were either to be fully abolished, or tightly regulated. In most countries they are legal but regulated.

Probably inspired by the dissenting judgments in a US Supreme Court case called *Adams v. Tanner*, the International Labour Organization's first ever Recommendation was targeted at fee charging agencies. The Unemployment Recommendation, 1919 (No.1), Art. 1 called for each member to,

> "take measures to prohibit the establishment of employment agencies which charge fees or which carry on their business for profit. Where such agencies already exist, it is further recommended that they be permitted to operate only under government licenses, and that all practicable measures be taken to abolish such agencies as soon as possible."

The Unemployment Convention, 1919, Art. 2 instead required the alternative of,

> "a system of free public employment agencies under the control of a central authority. Committees, which shall include representatives of employers and workers, shall be appointed to advise on matters concerning the carrying on of these agencies."

In 1933 the Fee-Charging Employment Agencies Convention (No.34) formally called for abolition. The exception was if the agencies were licensed and a fee scale was agreed in advance. In 1949 a new revised Convention (No.96) was produced. This kept the same scheme, but secured an 'opt out' (Art.2) for members that did not wish to sign up. Agencies were an increasingly entrenched part of the labor market. The United States did not sign up to the Conventions. The latest Convention, the Private Employment Agencies Convention, 1997 (No.181) takes a much softer stance and calls merely for regulation.

In most countries, agencies are regulated, for instance in the UK under the Employment Agencies Act 1973, or in Germany under the *Arbeitnehmerüberlassungsgesetz* (Employee Hiring Law of 1972).

Executive recruitment

Main article: Executive search

An executive-search firm is a type of employment agency that specializes in recruiting executive personnel for companies in various industries. This term may apply to job-search-consulting firms who charge job candidates a fee and who specialize in mid-to-upper-level executives. In the United States, some states require job-search-consulting firms to be licensed as employment agencies.

Some third-party recruiters work on their own, while others operate through an agency, acting as direct contacts between client companies and the job candidates they recruit. They can specialize in client relationships only (sales or business development), in finding candidates (recruiting or sourcing), or in both areas. Most recruiters tend to specialize in either permanent, full-time, direct-hire positions, or in contract positions, but occasionally in both. In an executive-search assignment, the employee-gaining client company – not the person being hired – pays the search firm its fee.

See also

- Temporary work
- UK agency worker law
- Talent agent
- Staffing
- Professional employer organization
- American Staffing Association
- Contingent workforce
- Payrolling
- ANPE, France's national employment agency

References

- DE Balducchi, RW Eberts, CJ O'Leary (eds), *Labour Exchange Policy in the United States* (Upjohn Institute 2004)
- P Craig, M Freedland, C Jacqueson and N Kountouris, *Public Employment Services and European Law* (2007)
- International Labour Office, *The role of private employment agencies in the functioning of labour markets* (Report VI 1994) International Labour Conference 81st Session
- R Kellogg, *The United States Employment Service* (University of Chicago Press 1933)
- T Martinez, *The Human Marketplace: An Examination of Private Employment Agencies* (Transaction 1976)
- JB Seymour, *The British Employment Exchange* (PS King & Son 1928)

Classified advertising

Classified advertising is a form of advertising which is particularly common in newspapers, online and other periodicals, e.g. free ads papers or Pennysavers. Classified advertising differs from standard advertising or business models in that it allows private individuals (not simply companies or corporate entities) to solicit sales for products and services.

Classified ads in a newspaper.

Overview

Classified advertising is usually text-only and can consist of as little as the type of item being sold and a telephone number to call for more information. It can also have much more detail, such as name to contact, address to contact or visit, a detailed description of the product or products ("pants and sweaters, size 10" as opposed to "clothing", "red 1996 Pontiac Grand Prix" as opposed to "automobile"). There are generally no pictures or other graphics within the advertisement, although sometimes a logo may be used.

Classified advertising is called such because it is generally grouped within the publication under headings classifying the product or service being offered (headings such as Accounting, Automobiles, Clothing, Farm Produce, For Sale, For Rent, etc.) and is grouped entirely in a distinct section of the periodical, which makes it distinct from display advertising, which often contains graphics or other art work and which is more typically distributed throughout a publication adjacent to editorial content.

A hybrid of the two forms — classified display advertising — may often be found, in which categorized advertisements with larger amounts of graphical detail can be found among the text listings of a classified advertising section in a publication. Business opportunities often use classifieds to sell their services, usually employing 1-800 numbers. Classified ads are also among the tools used by many companies in recruitment for available job opportunities.

Printed classified ads are typically just a few column lines in length, and they are often filled with abbreviations to save space and money.

Developments

In recent years the term "classified advertising" or "classified ads" has expanded from merely the sense of print advertisements in periodicals to include similar types of advertising on computer services, radio, and even television, particularly cable television but occasionally broadcast television as well, with the latter occurring typically very early in the morning hours.

Like most forms of printed media, the classified ad has found its way to the Internet.

Internet classified ads do not typically use per-line pricing models, so they tend to be longer. They are also more readily searchable unlike their offline brethren, tend to be local, and may foster a greater sense of urgency as a result of their daily structure and wider scope for audiences. Because of their self-policing nature and low cost structures, some companies offer free classifieds such as Craigslist, Loqqad, Kijiji, and Gumtree internationally. Other companies focus mainly on their local hometown region, while others blanket urban areas by using zip codes. Craigslist.org was one of the first online classified sites, and has grown to become the largest classified source, bringing in over 14 million unique visitors a month according to comScore Media Metrix. A number of online services called aggregators such as Trovit and sumavisos.com crawl and aggregate classifieds from sources such as blogs and RSS feeds, as opposed to relying on manually submitted listings.

Additionally, other companies provide online advertising services and tools to assist members in designing online ads using professional ad templates and then automatically distributing the finished ads to the various online ad directories as part of their service. In this sense these companies act as both an application service provider and a content delivery platform. Social classifieds is niche that is growing in online classified ads.

Statistics

In 2003, the market for classified ads in the United States was $15.9 billion (newspapers), $14.1 billion (online) according to market researcher Classified Intelligence. The worldwide market for classified ads in 2003 was estimated at over $100 billion. Perhaps due to a lack of reporting solidarity Market Statistics vary concerning the total market for internet classified ads. The Kelsey Research Group lists online classified ads as being worth $13.3 billion, while Jupiter Research provides a conservative appraisal of $2.6 billion (2005) and the Interactive Advertising Bureau lists the net worth of online classified revenue at $2.1 billion (April 2006).

Newspapers have continued their downward trend in classifieds revenue as internet classifieds grow. Classified advertising at some of the larger newspaper chains has dropped 14% to 20% in 2007 while traffic to classified sites has grown 23%.

As the online classified advertising sector develops, there is an increasing emphasis toward specialization. Vertical markets for classifieds are developing quickly along with the general marketplace for classifieds websites. Like search engines, classified websites are often vertical in nature with sites providing advertising platforms for niche markets of buyers of sellers.

See also

- Personal advertisement
- Tradio
- Newspaper display advertising

Job fair

A **job fair** is also referred commonly as a **career fair** or **career expo**. It is a fair or exposition for employers, recruiters and schools to meet with prospective job seekers. Expos usually include company or organization tables or booths where resumes can be collected and business cards can be exchanged. In the college setting, job fairs are commonly used for entry level job recruiting. Often sponsored by career centers, job fairs provide a convenient location for students to meet employers and perform first interviews. Electronic job fairs offer the same convenience online.

Job fairs are good places to meet many company representatives from corporations of all industries and sizes during a short period of time. Every job fair has a set of similar, basic elements or processes that require your attention. Job fair networking can be generally

described as the process of interacting with, obtaining contact details of, and getting to know corporate recruiters.

Prepare for Job Interviews

Job interview

A **job interview** is a process in which a potential employee is evaluated by an employer for prospective employment in their company, organization, or firm. During this process, the employer hopes to determine whether or not the applicant is suitable for the job.

Role

A job interview typically precedes the hiring decision, and is used to evaluate the candidate. The interview is usually preceded by the evaluation of submitted résumés from interested candidates, then selecting a small number of candidates for interviews. Potential job interview opportunities also include networking events and career fairs. The job interview is considered one of the most useful tools for evaluating potential employees. It also demands significant resources from the employer, yet has been demonstrated to be notoriously unreliable in identifying the optimal person for the job. An interview also allows the candidate to assess the corporate culture and demands of the job.

Multiple rounds of job interviews may be used where there are many candidates or the job is particularly challenging or desirable. Earlier rounds may involve fewer staff from the employers and will typically be much shorter and less in-depth. A common initial interview form is the phone interview, a job interview conducted over the telephone. This is especially common when the candidates do not live near the employer and has the advantage of keeping costs low for both sides.

Once all candidates have been interviewed, the employer typically selects the most desirable candidate and begins the negotiation of a job offer.

Process

A typical job interview has a single candidate meeting with between one and three persons representing the employer; the potential supervisor of the employee is usually involved in the interview process. A larger *interview panel* will often have a specialized human resources worker. While the meeting can be over in as little as 15 minutes, job interviews usually last less than two hours.

The bulk of the job interview will entail the interviewers asking the candidate questions about his or her job history, personality, work style and other factors relevant to the job. For instance, a common interview question is "What are your strengths and weaknesses?" In some ways, all questions are really subsets of one of three overarching questions "Can you do the job?" (strengths), "Will you love the job?" (motivation), "Can we stand working with you?" (fit). The candidate will usually be given a chance to ask any questions at the end of the interview. These questions are strongly encouraged since they allow the interviewee to acquire more information about the job and the company, but they can also demonstrate the candidate's strong interest in them.

Candidates for lower paid and lower skilled positions tend to have much simpler job interviews than do candidates for more senior positions. For instance, a lawyer's job interview will be much more demanding than that of a retail cashier. Most job interviews are formal; the larger the firm, the more formal and structured the interview will tend to be. Candidates generally dress slightly better than they would for work, with a suit (called an interview suit) being appropriate for a white-collar job interview.

Additionally, some professions have specific types of job interviews; for performing artists, this is an audition in which the emphasis is placed on the performance ability of the candidate.

In many companies, *assessment days* are increasingly being used, particularly for graduate positions, which may include analysis tasks, group activities, presentation exercises, and psychometric testing.

In recent years it has become increasingly common for employers to request job applicants who are successfully shortlisted to deliver one or more presentations at their interview. The purpose of the presentation in this setting may be to *either* demonstrate candidates' skills and abilities in presenting, or to highlight their knowledge of a given subject likely to relate closely to the job role for which they have applied. It is common for the applicant to be notified of the request for them to deliver a presentation along with their invitation to attend the interview. Usually applicants are only provided with a title for the presentation and a time limit which the presentation should not exceed.

Types

Behavioral

A common type of job interview in the modern workplace is the *behavioral interview* or *behavioral event interview*, also called a *competency-based interview*. This type of interview is based on the notion that a job candidate's previous behaviors are the best indicators of future performance. In behavioral interviews, the interviewer asks candidates to recall specific instances where they were faced with a set of circumstances, and how they reacted. Typical behavioral interview questions:

- "Tell me about a project you worked on where the requirements changed midstream. What did you do?"
- "Tell me about a time when you took the lead on a project. What did you do?"
- "Describe the worst project you worked on."
- "Describe a time you had to work with someone you didn't like."
- "Tell me about a time when you had to stick by a decision you had made, even though it made you very unpopular."

- "Give us an example of something particularly innovative that you have done that made a difference in the workplace."
- "What happened the last time you were late with a project?"
- "Have you ever witnessed a person doing something that you felt was against company policy. What did you do and why?"

A bad hiring decision nowadays can be immensely expensive for an organization—cost of the hire, training costs, severance pay, loss of productivity, impact on morale, cost of re-hiring, etc. (Gallup international places the cost of a bad hire as being 3.2 times the individual's salary). Studies indicate that 40% of new executives fail in their first 18 months in a new job. This has led to organizations investing in onboarding for their new employees to reduce these failure rates.

Case

Further information: Case interview

A case interview is an interview form used mostly by management consulting firms and investment banks in which the job applicant is given a question, situation, problem or challenge and asked to resolve the situation. The case problem is often a business situation or a business case that the interviewer has worked on in real life.

Panel

Another type of job interview found throughout the professional and academic ranks is the *panel interview*. In this type of interview the candidate is interviewed by a group of panelists representing the various stakeholders in the hiring process. Within this format there are several approaches to conducting the interview. Example formats include;

- Presentation format - The candidate is given a generic topic and asked to make a presentation to the panel. Often used in academic or sales-related interviews.
- Role format - Each panelist is tasked with asking questions related to a specific role of the position. For example one panelist may ask technical questions, another may ask management questions, another may ask customer service related questions etc.
- Skeet shoot format - The candidate is given questions from a series of panelists in rapid succession to test his or her ability to handle stress filled situations.

The benefits of the panel approach to interviewing include: time savings over serial interviewing, more focused interviews as there is often less time spend building rapport with small talk, and "apples to apples" comparison because each stake holder/interviewer/panelist gets to hear the same answers to the same questions.

Stress

Stress interviews are still in common use. One type of stress interview is where the employer uses a succession of interviewers (one at a time or *en masse*) whose mission is to intimidate the candidate and keep him/her off-balance. The ostensible purpose of this interview: to find out how the candidate handles stress. Stress interviews might involve testing an applicant's behavior in a busy environment. Questions about handling work overload, dealing with multiple projects, and handling conflict are typical.

Another type of stress interview may involve only a single interviewer who behaves in an uninterested or hostile manner. For example, the interviewer may not make eye contact, may roll his eyes or sigh at the candidate's answers, interrupt, turn his back, take phone calls during the interview, or ask questions in a demeaning or challenging style. The goal is to assess how the interviewee handles pressure or to purposely evoke emotional responses. This technique was also used in research protocols studying stress and type A (coronary-prone) behavior because it would evoke hostility and even changes in blood pressure and heart rate in study subjects. The key to success for the candidate is to de-personalize the process. The interviewer is acting a role, deliberately and calculatedly trying to "rattle the cage". Once the candidate realizes that there is nothing personal behind the interviewer's approach, it is easier to handle the questions with aplomb.

Example stress interview questions:

- Sticky situation: "If you caught a colleague cheating on his expenses, what would you do?"
- Putting you on the spot: "How do you feel this interview is going?"
- Popping the balloon: (deep sigh) "Well, if that's the best answer you can give ... " (shakes head) "Okay, what about this one ...?"
- Oddball question: "What would you change about the design of the hockey stick?"
- Doubting your veracity: "I don't feel like we're getting to the heart of the matter here. Start again - tell me what *really* makes you tick."

Candidates may also be asked to deliver a presentation as part of the selection process. The "Platform Test" method involves having the candidate make a presentation to both the selection panel and other candidates for the same job. This is obviously highly stressful and is therefore useful as a predictor of how the candidate will perform under similar circumstances on the job. Selection processes in academic, training, airline, legal and teaching circles frequently involve presentations of this sort.

Technical

Further information: Microsoft Interview

This kind of interview focuses on problem solving and creativity. The questions aim at your problem-solving skills and likely show your ability and creativity. Sometimes these interviews will be on a computer module with multiple-choice questions.

Telephone

Telephone interviews take place if a recruiter wishes to reduce the number of prospective candidates before deciding on a shortlist for face-to-face interviews. They also take place if a job applicant is a significant distance away from the premises of the hiring company, such as abroad or in another state or province.

Controversies

In many countries, employment equity laws forbid discrimination based on a number of classes, such as race, gender, age, sexual orientation, and marital status. Asking questions about these protected areas in a job interview is generally considered discriminatory, and constitutes an illegal hiring practice. Interviewers must pose their questions carefully in order to obtain the answers they want without instigating allegations of discrimination. Human Resources professionals generally learn these methods during their training and help to incorporate them into structured interview questions.

Validity and predictive power

There is extant data which puts into question the value of job interviews as a tool for selecting employees. Where the aim of a job interview is ostensibly to choose a candidate who will perform well in the job role, other methods of selection provide greater predictive power and often lower costs.[citation needed] Furthermore, given the unstructured approach of most interviews they often have almost no useful predictive power of employee success.

Honesty and integrity are attributes that can be very hard to determine using a formal job interview process: the competitive environment of the job interview may in fact promote dishonesty. Some experts on job interviews express a degree of cynicism towards the process. Wikipedia:Avoid weasel words

External links

- The Interview Process [1] by the Connecticut Department of Labor

Microsoft interview

The **Microsoft interview** is a job interview technique used by Microsoft to assess possible future Microsoft employees. It is significant because Microsoft's model was pioneering, and later picked up and developed by other companies, including Google.

Innovation

The Microsoft Interview was a pioneer in that it was about technical knowledge, problem solving and creativity as opposed to the goal and weaknesses interviews most companies used at the time. Initially based on Bill Gates' obsession with puzzles, many of the puzzles presented during interviews started off being Fermi problems, or sometimes logic problems, and have eventually transitioned over the years into questions relevant to programming: *[P]uzzles test competitive edge as well as intelligence. Like business or football, a logic puzzle divides the world into winners and losers. You either get the answer, or you don't... Winning has to matter.* Joel Spolsky phrased the problem as identifying people who are *smart and get things done* while separating them from *people who are smart but don't get things done* and *people who get things done but are not smart*

This model is now used widely in the IT Industry.

The positions

Microsoft hires both undergraduate college students ("college hires") and the more experienced ("industry hires"). For college hires, there's a focus on those with degrees in computer science, computer engineering, electrical engineering or systems engineering for the three main technical positions of Software Development Engineer (SDE), Software Development Engineer in Test (SDET) and Program Manager (PM).

Microsoft also hires for non-technical positions and those who have an MBA. The interview would not be a technical one.

College Recruitment Phases

Microsoft College Recruitment practices can be divided into phases.

Résumé/College Fair

Microsoft recruits heavily from college campuses in the United States.

The interviewing process typically begins with college students attending a career fair on campus and submitting a résumé to recruiters. The campus fair and accompanying on-campus information session about the company gives students the opportunity to find out more about what Microsoft does, and to ask questions of current employees.

First Interview

After the résumés have been collected, a select number of students are contacted for a first-round interview usually held on the candidate's college campus or over the telephone with a single recruiter. The first-round interview can last for about thirty to forty five minutes.

The candidate is initially asked to fill out an application form prior to the interview detailing work-location (Redmond, Silicon Valley, North Carolina, Nebraska) and work-type preferences (Business initiatives, media center/gaming, operating system, etc.).

During this interview the recruiter attempts to determine if the candidate will be able to flourish at Microsoft. After the interview, the recruiter will consider whether Microsoft's current business needs and the candidate's qualifications and interests are compatible.

Questions

Some examples of questions that the recruiter will keep in mind or ask a candidate include:

- What types of projects (academic or otherwise) have inspired you in the past?
- What are some self-directed missions that may have influenced your career direction?
- Did you have a moment of epiphany when you KNEW what you wanted to be when you grew up?
- How does Microsoft fit into your vision?
- What are some things that excite and motivate you?
- What are some examples of poorly/well-designed software? What makes the software this way and how would you change it?

Microsoft expects that the candidate know its various businesses and product groups, and come prepared to speak in-depth about their résumé in addition to asking thoughtful questions.

Post First Interview

The candidate can generally expect to receive the results of the first-round interview from the recruiter within about 2 to 3 weeks of the interview date. If the first-round interview was successful, the candidate is contacted by a Microsoft recruiting co-ordinator to arrange a mutually acceptable date for the second-round interview.

Travel and lodging arrangements are then processed and finalized.

Second Interview

If candidates successfully complete the first-round interview, the third phase is the second-round interview, which is held in Microsoft's headquarters located in Redmond, Washington.

The maximum length of the candidate's interview trip can be up to three days and two nights, which includes one day to interview and one day to sight-see.

Candidates interviewing for the program manager position can be expected to answer detailed design questions that test the candidate's creative ability and focus on customers. The candidate is expected to provide reasons for features added to products designed and include explanations as to why a customer might want or need a particular feature.

Candidates interviewing for the SDE and SDET positions can be expected to answer detailed coding and algorithm questions.

Many questions asked are purposely ambiguous and/or abstract. It is expected that the candidate ask thought-provoking questions of the interviewer in order to better answer the question. The candidate is normally given a marker, eraser, and a whiteboard to record his/her solutions and ideas to questions. The interviewer observes how the candidate attempts to solve a problem and follows the candidate's thought processes.

The interview day usually comprises meeting with about three to five different employees within Microsoft. A typical schedule might include two interviews in the morning, one lunch interview, and two interviews in the afternoon. The lunch interview can take place in one of Microsoft's various in-house cafeterias or in a restaurant off-campus. In most cases the candidate will interview with two different product teams within a single product group or two entirely different product groups (Microsoft site FAQ 2006). It depends on the current business needs of Microsoft at the time of the interview and which needs best fit the candidate's skill set and interests. The candidate is generally notified on the day of the interview as to which position he/she will be interviewing for if the candidate is interviewing for Software Development Engineer, Software Development Engineer in Test, or Program Manager Positions.

Following each interview with the candidate, the interviewer will email the complete set of interviewers with their feedback on the candidate. This email generally begins with a summary "Hire" or "No hire" assessment. The last interviewer to see the candidate is special, and referred to as the "As

Appropriate" or "As Ap". This person, generally the most senior person among the set of interviewers, will only see the candidate if the email feedback on that candidate thus far has been generally positive, or at least split between "Hire" and "No Hire" assessments. The "As Appropriate" interviewer often makes the final call as to whether the candidate will receive an offer.

Post Second Interview

After the second-round interview the candidate is asked to submit a reimbursement form for any expenses incurred during the trip to Redmond (i.e. taxi travel and meals). The candidate then generally receives an e-mail or phone call detailing the outcome of the second-round interview. If selected, an offer is made and the candidate is given a list of starting dates to decide on whether to accept based on any other pending offers.

Further information

Interview questions

The questions asked during the Microsoft Interview are crafted to determine a candidate's problem solving, coding and design abilities. Eccentric questions (such as *Which of the fifty states would you remove?*) test a candidate's ability to come to a decision and articulate it. Candidates answering questions should consider the use of technology in the present and future, and User scenarios. Some questions involve projects that the candidate has worked on in the past.

The Microsoft Interview is intended to seek out creative thinkers and those who can adapt their solutions to rapidly changing and dynamic scenarios.

Below is a small sample of questions that a candidate might be asked to answer during the second-round interview:

- Design a cellphone for a blind person.
- Design a music system for a car. What are the features? Draw a picture.
- Design a GPS navigation unit for a hiker
- Design a communication device for Canadian park rangers.
- Design a remote control for an automatic window-blind system.
- Design TV Remote Control with Two Buttons.
- Design a coffee maker that will be used by astronauts.
- Design an alarm clock.
- Design an alarm clock for a blind person.
- Design a search function
- Design a website for a library
- Design an ATM for children
- What method would you use to look up a word in a dictionary?

- What are examples of poorly designed software?
- Design an instant messaging system.
- I am your grandmother. Describe what MATLAB is to me.
- How would you explain what a database is to a 5-year-old?
- How would you explain computer networking to a kindergarten kid?
- What is your favourite software, and how would you improve it?
- Write code for an electronic messaging board. What happens when a user logs on?
- Develop an algorithm for selecting objects in Visio.
- Tell me about a time when you made a decision and later found out that it was incorrect. What did you do to resolve the issue?
- Suppose you are one week away from the product shipping date and discover a bug in your software. What do you do?
- You have a linked list and don't know how long it is; how do you find the middle of it?
- How would you test a keyboard?
- How would you test a pen?
- Write code for finding a duplicate in an array.
- Write code that returns the length of a string without using any built-in functions.
- Reverse a Singly Linked List with and without using Recursion.
- Determine if a Binary Search Tree is well formed.
- Reverse every word in a String (*abc def* becomes *cba fed*).
- Write a function that returns the angle between the hour and the minute hands of a clock, given input of the time.
- Write a function that takes a string consisting of numeral characters and returns all possible alpha character strings of same length as input that correspond to the keypad of a typical telephone.
- Imagine you have a closet full of shirts. It's very hard to find a shirt. So what can you do to organize your shirts for easy retrieval?
- How would you test an elevator?
- How would you test a vending machine?
- How would you test a program that takes in two points and outputs the distance between the two points?
- Test the Windows scroll bar.
- Switch every pair of words in a string ("ab cd ef gh" becomes "cd ab gh ef")
- Write the function for strstr function (finding a substring inside a string)
- Reverse the order of words in a string ("ab cd ef gh" becomes "gh ef cd ab")
- Write the function for string comparison. How would you test it?
- Write a function to zero all duplicate values in an integer array. How would you test it?
- Write a function that compares two strings and returns a third string containing only the letters that appear in both.

Interview resources

Microsoft provides a list of suggested reading to prepare for the interview. A sampling is given below:

- *Cracking the Coding Interview*, Gayle Laakmann 2008
- *Writing Solid Code*, Steve Maguire
- *Code Complete*, Steve McConnell
- *Testing Computer Software*, Cem Kaner
- *All I Really Need to Know in Business I Learned at Microsoft*, Julie Bick
- *Business @ the Speed of Thought*, Bill Gates
- *The Road Ahead*, Bill Gates
- *Algorithms in C*, Robert Sedgewick, eds. . Addison-Wesley, 1990.
- *Essential .NET Vol 1 The Common Language Runtime*, Don Box Addison-Wesley, 2003.
- *Lessons Learned in Software Testing*, Cem Kaner, James Bach, Bret Pettichord Wiley Computer Publishing 2002
- *Mythical Man-Month Anniversary Edition*, Frederick P. Brooks, Jr. Addison-Wesley, 1995
- *Introduction to Algorithms Second Edition*, Thomas H. Cormen, Charles E. Leiserson, Ronald L. Rivest, and Cliff Stein MIT Press, 2001
- *The Art of Computer Programming*, Donald Knuth Addison-Wesley

References

- Microsoft College Careers. The Interview — First Round [1]. Retrieved from the World Wide Web on January 16, 2006.
- Job Interviews Get Creative, NPR 2003 [2]. Retrieved from the World Wide Web on January 16, 2006.

External links

- Microsoft Interview Questions [3]

Unemployment Benefits

Unemployment benefits

Economics

General categories
Microeconomics · Macroeconomics History of economic thought Methodology · Heterodox approaches
Techniques
Mathematical · Econometrics Experimental · National accounting
Fields and subfields
Behavioral · Cultural · Evolutionary Growth · Development · History International · Economic systems Monetary and Financial economics Public and Welfare economics Health · Education · Welfare Population · Labour · Managerial Business · Information · Game theory Industrial organization · Law Agricultural · Natural resource Environmental · Ecological Urban · Rural · Regional · Geography
Lists
Journals · Publications Categories · Topics · Economists
The economy: concept and history
Business and Economics Portal

Unemployment benefits are payments made by the state or other authorized bodies to unemployed people. Benefits may be based on a compulsory para-governmental insurance system. Depending on the jurisdiction and the status of the person, those sums may be small, covering only basic needs (thus a form of basic welfare), or may compensate the lost time proportionally to the previous earned salary. They often are part of a larger social security scheme.

Unemployment benefits are generally given only to those registering as unemployed, and often on conditions ensuring that they seek work and do not currently have a job.

In some countries, a significant proportion of unemployment benefits are distributed by trade/labor unions, an arrangement known as the Ghent system.

Argentina

In Argentina, successive administrations have used a variety of passive and active labor market interventions to protect workers against the consequences of economic shocks and the government's key institutional response to combat the increase in poverty and unemployment created by the crisis was the launch of an active unemployment assistance program called Plan Jefas y Jefes de Hogar Desocupados (Program for Unemployed Heads of Households).

External links

- [1] Unemployment Assistance and Transition to Employment in Argentina

Australia

Main article: Social Security (Australia)

In Australia, social security benefits, including unemployment benefits, are funded through the income tax system. There is no compulsory national unemployment insurance fund, rather, benefits are provided for in the annual Federal Budget by the National Treasury and are administrated and distributed throughout the nation by Centrelink. Benefit rates are indexed to the Consumer Price Index and are adjusted twice a year according to the amount of underlying inflation or deflation.

There are two types of payment available to those experiencing unemployment. The first, called Youth Allowance, is paid to young people aged 16–20 (or 15, if deemed independent by Centrelink). Youth Allowance is also paid to full-time students aged 16–24, and to full-time Australian Apprenticeship workers aged 16–24. People aged below 18 who have not completed their High School education, are usually required to be in full-time education, undertaking an apprenticeship or doing training to be eligible for Youth Allowance. For single under 18 year olds living at home the basic rate is AUD$91.60 per week. For over 18 to 20 years olds living at home this increases to AUD$110.15 per week. For those aged 18–20 not living at home the rate is AUD$167.35 per week. There are special rates for those with partners and/or children.

The second kind of payment is called Newstart Allowance and is paid to unemployed people over the age of 21 and under the pension eligibility age. To get Newstart you must be unemployed, be prepared to enter into an Employment Pathway Plan (previously called an Activity Agreement) by which you agree to undertake certain activities to increase your opportunities for employment, are an Australian Resident and satisfy the income test (which limits weekly income to AUD$32 per week before benefits begin to reduce, until your income reaches AUD$397.42 per week at which point no unemployment benefits are paid) and the assets test (you can have assets of up to AUD$161,500 if you own a home before the allowance begins to reduce and $278,500 if you do not own a home). The rate of Newstart allowance as at the 12th January 2010 for single people without children is AU$228 per week, paid fortnightly. (This does not include supplemental payments such as Rent Assistance.) Different rates apply to people with partners and/or children.

The system in Australia is designed to support citizens no matter how long they have been unemployed. This has been criticized by some conservative commentators, who allege that welfare generates a 'culture of welfare dependence'. In recent years the former Coalition government under John Howard has increased the requirements of the Activity Agreement, providing for controversial schemes such as Work for the Dole, which requires that people on benefits for 6 months or longer work voluntarily for a community organization to increase their skills and job prospects. Since the Labor government under Kevin Rudd was elected in 2008, the length of unemployment before one is required to fulfil the requirements of the Activity Agreement (which has been renamed the Employment Pathway Plan) has increased from six to twelve months. There are other options available as alternatives to the Work for the Dole scheme, such as undertaking part-time work or study and training, the basic premise of the Employment Pathway Plan being to keep the welfare recipient active and involved in seeking full-time work.

For people renting their accommodation, unemployment benefits are supplemented by Rent Assistance, which, for single people as at the 12th January, 2010, begins to be paid when the weekly rent is more than AUD$49.70. Rent Assistance is paid as a proportion of total rent paid (to be precise, 75 cents in the dollar over $49.70 up to the maximum). The maximum amount of rent assistance payable is AU$55.90 per week, and is paid when the total weekly rent exceeds AU$124.24 per week. Different rates apply to people with partners and/or children, or who are sharing accommodation.

External links

- Centrelink web-site [2]

Canada

In Canada the system now known as Employment Insurance was formerly called Unemployment Insurance until 1996 when it was changed due to perceived negative connotations. Canadian workers pay premiums of 1.73% of insured earnings in return for benefits if they lose their jobs. Employers contribute 1.4 times the value of employee premiums. Since 1990, there is no government contribution to this fund. The amount a person receives and how long they can stay on EI varies with their previous salary, how long they were working, and the unemployment rate in their area. The EI system is managed by Service Canada, a service delivery network reporting to the Minister of Human Resources and Social Development Canada.

A bit over half of EI benefits are paid in Ontario and the Western provinces but EI is especially important in the Atlantic provinces, which have higher rates of unemployment. Many Atlantic workers are also employed in seasonal work such as fishing, forestry or tourism and go on EI over the winter when there is no work. There are special rules for fishermen making it easier for them to collect EI. EI also pays for maternity and parental leave, compassionate care leave, and illness coverage. The program also pays for retraining programs (EI Part II) through labour market agreements with the Canadian provinces.

An unemployment insurance program was first attempted in 1935 during the Great Depression by the government of R.B. Bennett. It was, however, ruled unconstitutional by the Supreme Court of Canada as unemployment was judged to be an insurance matter falling under provincial responsibility. After a constitutional amendment was agreed to by the provinces, a reference to "Unemployment Insurance" was added to the matters falling under federal authority under the Constitution Act, 1867, and the first Canadian system was adopted in 1940. Because of these problems Canada was the last major Western country to bring in an employment insurance system. It was extended dramatically by Pierre Trudeau in 1971 making it much easier to get. The system was sometimes called the 10/42, because one had to work for 10 weeks to get benefits for the other 42 weeks of the year. It was also in 1971 that the UI program was first opened up to maternity and sickness benefits, for 15 weeks in each case.

The generosity of the Canadian UI program was progressively reduced after the adoption of the 1971 UI Act. At the same time, the federal government gradually reduced its financial contribution, eliminating it entirely by 1990. The EI system was again cut by the Progressive Conservatives in 1990 and 1993, then by the Liberals in 1994 and 1996. Amendments made it harder to qualify by increasing the time needed to be worked, although seasonal claimants (who work long hours over short periods) turned out to gain from the replacement, in 1996, of weeks by hours to qualify. The ratio of beneficiaries to unemployed, after having stood at around 40 percent for many years, has recently reached close to 50% (end of 2009). Many unemployed persons are not covered for benefits (e.g. the self-employed), while others may have exhausted their benefits or did not work long enough to qualify. However, it is noted that 80 percent of insured job-losers do initially receive EI benefits in Canada. The length of time one could take EI has also been cut repeatedly. The 1994 and 1996 changes contributed to a sharp fall in Liberal support in the Atlantic provinces in the 1997 election.

In 2001, the federal government increased parental leave from 10 to 35 weeks and allowed workers to take EI for compassionate care leave while caring for a dying relative. Total EI spending is projected at $22.7 billion for 2010 (figures in Canadian dollars).

A significant part of the federal fiscal surplus of the Jean Chrétien and Paul Martin years came from the EI system. Premiums were reduced much less than falling expenditures - producing, from 1994 onwards, EI surpluses of several billion dollars per year, which were added to general government revenue. The cumulative EI surplus stood at $57 billion at March 31, 2008, nearly four times the amount needed to cover the extra costs paid during a recession. This drew criticism from Opposition parties and from business and labour groups, and has remained a recurring issue of the public debate. The Conservative Party, after voicing much the same criticism while in opposition, chose not to recognize existing EI surpluses after being elected in 2006. Instead, the Conservative government adopted in 2008 and 2009 legislation freezing the EI surplus indefinitely and putting EI premiums on a pay-as-you-go basis, so that - starting in 2011 - they will fluctuate in line with changes in unemployment levels. On December 11, 2008, the Supreme Court of Canada rejected a court challenge launched against the federal government by two Quebec unions, who argued that EI funds had been misappropriated by the government.

A slang term often used for EI is "Pogey". An example of the use of this term would be "Just keep working until you get your pogey", or "my husband is on pogey".

External links

- [3] History of UI in Canada, since 1930s
- [4] Canadian Government Site for EI
- [5] Canadian Government Site for Maternity and Parental Benefits
- [6] Canadian Employment Insurance Calculator
- [7] Library of Parliament publication on EI premiums
- CBC Digital Archives - On The Dole: Employment Insurance in Canada [8]

China

The level of benefit is set between the minimum wage and the minimum living allowance by individual provinces, autonomous regions and municipalities.

Greece

Unemployment benefits in Greece are administered through OAED (Labor Force Employment Organization) and are available only to laid-off salaried workers with full employment and social security payments during the previous two years. The self-employed do not qualify, and neither do those with other sources of income. The monthly benefit is fixed at the "55% of 25 minimum daily wages", and is currently 454 euros per month, with a 10% increase for each under-age child.

Ireland

People aged 18 and over and who are unemployed in Ireland can apply for either the **Jobseeker's Allowance** (*Liúntas do Lucht Cuardaigh Fostaíochta*) or the **Jobseeker's Benefit** (*Sochar do Lucht Cuardaigh Fostaíochta*). Both are paid by the Department of Social Protection and are nicknamed "the dole".

The standard payment is €196 (maximum rate 2010) per week. Payments can be increased if the unemployed has dependants. For each adult dependent, another €135.60 (maximum rate 2009) is added; and for each child dependent, another €26.00 (maximum rate 2009) is added.

There are more benefits available to unemployed people, usually on a special or specific basis. Benefits include the *Rent Supplement*, the *Mortgage Interest Supplement, Fuel Allowance* and the *Smokeless Fuel Allowance*, among others. People on a low income (which includes those on JA/JB) are entitled to a Medical Card (although this must be applied for separately from the Health Service Executive) which provides free health care, optical care, dental care, aural care, and prescription drugs (as opposed to subsidised services like non medical-card holders). Education (at all levels) is free to all, not just the unemployed.

To qualify for Jobseekers Allowance, claimants must satisfy the "Habitual Residence Condition": they must have been legally in the state (or the Common Travel Area) for two years or have another good reason (such as lived abroad and are returning to Ireland after become unemployed or deported). This condition does not apply to Jobseekers Benefit (which is based on Social Insurance payments).

More information on each benefit can be found here:

- Jobseeker's Allowance [9]
- Jobseeker's Benefit [10]

Italy

Main article: Unemployment benefits in Italy

Unemployment benefits in Italy consists mainly in cash transfers based on contributions (*indennità di disoccupazione*), up to the 40 percent of the previous wages for up to seven months. Other measures are:

- Redundancy Fund (*Cassa integrazione guadagni*, CIG): cash benefits provided as shock absorbers to those workers who are suspended or who work only for reduced time due to temporary difficulties of their factories, aiming to help the factories in financial difficulties, by relieving them from the costs of unused workforce
- Solidarity Contracts (*Contratti di solidarietà*): in the same cases granting CIG benefits, companies can sign contracts with reduced work time, to avoid dismissing redundancy workers. The state will

grant to those workers the 60 percent of the lost part of the wage.

- Mobility allowances (*Indennità di mobilità*),: if the Redundancy Fund doesn't allow the company to re-establish a good financial situation, the workers can be entitled to mobility allowances. Other companies are provided incentives for employing them.

In the Italian unemployment insurance system all the measures are income-related, and they have an average decommodification level. The basis for entitlement is always employment, with more specific conditions for each case, and the provider is quite always the state. An interesting feature worthy to be discussed is that the Italian system takes in consideration also the economic situation of the employers, and aims as well at relieving them from the costs of crisis.

New Zealand

Main article: Social welfare in New Zealand

In New Zealand, these benefits provide income support for people who are looking for work or training for work through Work and Income, a service of the Ministry of Social Development

To qualify, a person needs to be aged 18 or over, or aged 16–17 and living with a partner and children they support and:

- have continually lived in New Zealand for two years or more
- not working full-time, but actively looking for a full-time job and able to start work now.
- a person may still qualify if he/she is a full-time trainee on an approved work related course. The course must usually be less than 12 weeks long to qualify. People must still take steps to meet the job search requirements.

A person who applies for the benefit may be asked to develop a Job Seeker Agreement with Work and Income where he/she agrees to look for work or prepare for work

If the applicant has a partner they may be included in the benefit and may also be asked to develop a Job Seeker Agreement with Work and Income. They may also need to:

- look for full-time work (30 hours a week or more) if applicant has no children at home or applicant's youngest child is aged 14 or older or
- look for part-time work (15 hours a week or more) if applicant's youngest child is aged 6–13 or come to annual planning meetings and perhaps do things to help prepare for work if applicant's youngest child is less than six years old.

In New Zealand the benefit is $158.65 weekly after tax for single person who is 20–24 years. A married, de-facto or civil union couple with or without children receive $317.30 per week after tax ($158.65 each). Single persons 25 years or over get $190.39 per week after tax. The benefit payment can reduce due to any income the person or their partner earns.

External links

- Work and Income web-site [11]

Sweden

Main article: Unemployment benefits in Sweden

Sweden uses the Ghent system, under which a significant proportion of unemployment benefits are distributed by unions. Unemployment benefits are divided into a voluntary scheme with income related compensation up to a certain level and a comprehensive scheme that provides a lower level of basic support. The voluntary scheme requires a minimum of 12 months membership and a certain degree of employment during that time before any claims can be made. Employers pay a fee on top of the pre-tax income of their employees, which together with membership fees, fund the scheme (see Unemployment funds in Sweden).

The maximum unemployment benefit is (as of July 2007) SEK 680 per day (SEK 14,960 per month). During the first 200 days the unemployed will receive 80 percent of his or her normal income during the last 12 months. From day 201-300 this goes down to 70 percent and from day 301-450 the insurance covers 65 percent of the normal income (only available for parents to children under the age of 18). In Sweden tax is paid on unemployment benefits, so the unemployed will get a maximum of about SEK 10,000 per month during the first 100 days (depending on the municipality tax rate). In other currencies this means a maximum of approximately £730, $1,650, or €1,100, each month after tax. Private insurance is also available, mainly through professional organizations, to provide income related compensation that otherwise exceeds the ceiling of the scheme. The comprehensive scheme is funded by tax.

Saudi Arabia

Saudi Arabia is an economic welfare state with free medical care and unemployment benefits. However, the country relies not on taxation but mainly oil revenues to maintain the social and economic services to its populace.

External links

- Social Services of Saudi Arabia [12]

United Kingdom

Main article: Jobseeker's Allowance

Jobseeker's Allowance rates

JSA for a single person is changed annually, and at June 29, 2009 the maximum payable was £65.45 per week for a person aged over 25, £51.85 per week for a person aged 18–24. The rules for couples where both are unemployed are more complex, but a maximum of £102.75 per week is payable, dependent on age and other factors. Income-based JSA is reduced for people with savings of over £6,000, by a reduction of £1 per week per £250 of savings, up to £16,000. People with savings of over £16,000 are not able to get IB-JSA at all. The British system provides rent payments as part of a separate scheme called Local Housing Allowance. Unemployed persons are able to submit Enduring Power of Attorney/Lasting Power of Attorney submissions free of charge saving £120 each.

History and etymology

Unemployment benefits were first instituted in 1911. Over 2 million people were relying on the payments by 1921, as the United Kingdom was experiencing economic hardship after World War I.

To receive unemployment benefit is commonly referred to as "being on the dole", "dole" being an archaic expression meaning "one's allotted portion", from the synonymous Old English word *dāl*.

United States

Unemployment compensation is money received from the United States and a state by a worker who has become unemployed through no fault of their own. In the United States, this compensation is classified as a type of social welfare benefit. According to the Internal Revenue Code, these types of benefits are to be included in a taxpayer's gross income.

Federal-State joint programs

Wisconsin originated the idea of unemployment insurance (UI) in the U.S. in 1932. In the United States, there are 50 state **unemployment insurance** programs plus one each in the District of Columbia and Puerto Rico. Through the Social Security Act of 1935, the Federal Government of the United States effectively encouraged the individual states to adopt unemployment insurance plans.

Unemployment insurance is a federal-state program jointly financed through federal and state employer payroll taxes (federal and state UI taxes). Generally, employers must pay both state and federal unemployment taxes if:

> (1) they pay wages to employees totaling $1,500 or more in any quarter of a calendar year; or,

(2) they had at least one employee during any day of a week during 20 weeks in a calendar year, regardless of whether the weeks were consecutive. However, some state laws differ from the federal law.

To facilitate this program, the U.S. Congress passed the Federal Unemployment Tax Act (FUTA), which authorizes the Internal Revenue Service (IRS) to collect an annual federal employer tax used to fund state workforce agencies. FUTA covers the costs of administering the Unemployment Insurance and Job Service programs in all states. In addition, FUTA pays one-half of the cost of extended unemployment benefits (during periods of high unemployment) and provides for a fund from which states may borrow, if necessary, to pay benefits. As originally established, the states paid the federal government.

The FUTA tax rate was originally three percent of taxable wages collected from employers who employed at least four employees, and employers could deduct up to 90 percent of the amount due if they paid taxes to a state to support a system of unemployment insurance which met Federal standards, but the rules have changed as follows. The FUTA tax rate is now 6.2 percent of taxable wages of employees who meet both the above and following criteria, and the taxable wage base is the first $7,000 paid in wages to each employee during a calendar year. Employers who pay the state unemployment tax on a timely basis receive an offset credit of up to 5.4 percent regardless of the rate of tax they pay their state. Therefore, the net FUTA tax rate is generally 0.8 percent (6.2 percent - 5.4 percent), for a maximum FUTA tax of $56.00 per employee, per year (.008 X $7,000 = $56.00). State law determines individual state unemployment insurance tax rates. In the United States, unemployment insurance tax rates use experience rating.

Within the above constraints, the individual states and territories raise their own contributions and run their own programs. The federal government sets broad guidelines for coverage and eligibility, but states vary in how they determine benefits and eligibility.

Federal rules are drawn by the United States Department of Labor, Employment and Training Administration. For most states, the maximum period for receiving benefits is 26 weeks. There is an extended benefit program (authorized through the Social Security Acts) that may be triggered by state economic conditions. Congress has often passed temporary programs to extend benefits during economic recessions. This was done with the Temporary Extended Unemployment Compensation (TEUC) program in 2002-2003, which has since expired, and remained in force through June 2, 2010, with the Extended Unemployment Compensation 2008 legislation. In July, legislation that provides an extension of federal extended unemployment benefits through November was signed by the President. The extension restored unemployment benefits to the 2.3 million unemployed Americans who had run out of basic unemployment benefits. However, the current extensions in place expire on November 30 unless legislation is passed by Congress providing for an additional extension. Congress is considering extending the Temporary Extended Unemployment Compensation program again.

The federal government lends money to the states for unemployment insurance when the states run short of funds. In general, this can happen when the unemployment rate is high. The need for loans can be exacerbated when a state cuts taxes and increases benefits. All loans must be repaid with interest.

Congressional actions to massively increase penalties for states incurring large debts for unemployment benefits led to state fiscal crises in the 1980s.[citation needed]

Because it is a joint federal/state program run by the states, taxing business for the benefit of labor, the politics of unemployment insurance are very complex.

Economic functioning

The Unemployment Insurance (UI) program helps counter economic fluctuations. When the economy grows, UI program revenue rises through increased tax revenues while UI program spending falls as fewer workers are unemployed. The effect of collecting more taxes than are spent dampens demand in the economy.[citation needed] This also creates a surplus of funds or a "cushion" of available funds for the UI program to draw upon during a recession. In a recession, UI tax revenue falls and UI program spending rises as more workers lose their jobs and receive UI benefits. The increased amount of UI payments to unemployed workers puts additional funds into the economy and dampens the effect of earnings losses.[citation needed]

Eligibility and amount

Americans out of work who do not qualify for unemployment insurance include part-time, temporary, and self-employed workers.

Generally, the worker must be unemployed through no fault of his/her own (generally through lay-offs). Unemployment benefits are based on reported covered quarterly earnings. The amount of earnings and the number of quarters worked are used to determine the length and value of the unemployment benefit. The average weekly payment is 36 percent of the individual's average weekly wage.

Application process

It generally takes two weeks for benefit payments to begin, the first being a "waiting week", which is not reimbursed, and the second being the time lag between eligibility for the program and the first benefit actually being paid.

To begin a claim, the unemployed worker must apply for benefits through a state unemployment agency. In certain instances, the employer initiates the process. Generally, the certification includes affected person affirming that they are "able and available for work", the amount of any part-time earnings they may have had, and whether they are actively seeking work. These certifications are usually accomplished either by internet or via an interactive voice response telephone call, but in a few states may be by mail. After receiving an application, the state will notify the individual if they qualify and the rate they will receive every week. The state will also review the reason for separation from employment. Many states require the individual to periodically certify that the conditions of the benefits are still met.

Current data

Each Thursday, the Department of Labor issues the *Unemployment Insurance Weekly Claims Report*. Its headline number is the seasonally adjusted estimate for the initial claims for unemployment for the previous week in the United States. This statistic, because of its timeliness, is an important indicator of the health of the labor market, and more broadly, the vigor of the overall economy.

Taxation

The argument for taxation of social welfare benefits is that they result in a realized gain for a taxpayer. The argument against taxation is that the benefits are generally less than the federal poverty level.

Unemployment compensation has been taxable by the federal government since 1987. Code Section 85 deemed unemployment compensation included in gross income. Federal taxes are not withheld from unemployment compensation at the time of payment unless requested by the recipient using Form W-4V.

In 2003, Rep. Philip English introduced legislation to repeal the taxation of unemployment compensation, but the legislation did not advance past committee. Most states with income tax consider unemployment compensation to be taxable.

Prior to 1987, unemployment compensation amounts were excluded from federal gross income.

For the US Federal tax year of 2009, as a result of the signing of the American Recovery and Reinvestment Act of 2009 signed by Barack Obama on February 17, 2009 the first $2,400 worth of unemployment income received during the 'tax year' of 2009 will be exempted from being considered as taxable income on the Federal level, when American taxpayers file their 2009 IRS tax return paperwork in early 2010.

Work sharing

Employers have the option of reducing work hours to part-time for many employees instead of laying off some of them and retaining only full-time workers. Employees in 18 states can then receive unemployment payments for the hours they are no longer working.

See also

- Job sharing
- 99ers
- Unemployment
- Unemployment extension
- Social rights
- Hartz concept
- HIRE Act
- Parental leave
- Reserve army of labour
- Labour power
- Compensation of employees
- Lorenz curve
- Social security
- J. S. Woodsworth
- Social insurance

References

- Bojas George J., *Labor Economics*, Second edition, 2002, McGraw-Hill.

External links

- Government site: Latest month's unemployment rate report [1]
- Find it Fast, Find it Free - Direct links to your state's unemployment insurance benefits [2]
- Government site: One-Stop Career Centers - in each state [3]
- State Employment Offices by State [1]
- Text of the California Unemployment Insurance Code [4]
- Economic Policy Institute [5] - To calculate the unemployment insurance benefits you might receive in the United States (based on ^{2004} rates)
- A guide to collecting unemployment Benefits in the United States of America [6]
- Office of the Public Guardian [7]
- First $2,400 of Unemployment Benefits Tax Free for 2009 [8]

- Guide to Unemployment Insurance Eligibility in the UK [9]

Article Sources and Contributors

Job hunting *Source*: http://en.wikipedia.org/?oldid=390190008 *Contributors*: Beland

Employment website *Source*: http://en.wikipedia.org/?oldid=390296110 *Contributors*: MrOllie

Job wrapping *Source*: http://en.wikipedia.org/?oldid=382427173 *Contributors*: Bearcat

CareerBuilder *Source*: http://en.wikipedia.org/?oldid=382371574 *Contributors*: 1 anonymous edits

Incruit *Source*: http://en.wikipedia.org/?oldid=366544782 *Contributors*:

Monster.com *Source*: http://en.wikipedia.org/?oldid=385350389 *Contributors*: PLA y Grande Covián

Craigslist *Source*: http://en.wikipedia.org/?oldid=390310821 *Contributors*:

LinkedIn *Source*: http://en.wikipedia.org/?oldid=390561789 *Contributors*: 1 anonymous edits

Yahoo! HotJobs *Source*: http://en.wikipedia.org/?oldid=381132122 *Contributors*: Rillian

Simply Hired *Source*: http://en.wikipedia.org/?oldid=380378784 *Contributors*:

Indeed.com *Source*: http://en.wikipedia.org/?oldid=390353179 *Contributors*:

FINS.com *Source*: http://en.wikipedia.org/?oldid=373140874 *Contributors*: AlexandergordonNYC

Twitter *Source*: http://en.wikipedia.org/?oldid=390679903 *Contributors*: Tmorton166

Facebook *Source*: http://en.wikipedia.org/?oldid=390433500 *Contributors*: SQGibbon

AdWords *Source*: http://en.wikipedia.org/?oldid=389056749 *Contributors*: 1 anonymous edits

Video resume *Source*: http://en.wikipedia.org/?oldid=385291666 *Contributors*: 1 anonymous edits

YouTube *Source*: http://en.wikipedia.org/?oldid=390508765 *Contributors*: Ianmacm

Employment agency *Source*: http://en.wikipedia.org/?oldid=376278779 *Contributors*: 1 anonymous edits

Classified advertising *Source*: http://en.wikipedia.org/?oldid=390556511 *Contributors*: EncMstr

Job fair *Source*: http://en.wikipedia.org/?oldid=384392273 *Contributors*: Prolog

Job interview *Source*: http://en.wikipedia.org/?oldid=387935511 *Contributors*:

Microsoft interview *Source*: http://en.wikipedia.org/?oldid=389374762 *Contributors*: Versageek

Unemployment benefits *Source*: http://en.wikipedia.org/?oldid=389844310 *Contributors*: 1 anonymous edits

Image Sources, Licenses and Contributors

Image:Craigslist.svg *Source*: http://bibliocm.bibliolabs.com/mwAnon/index.php?title=File:Craigslist.svg *License*: Trademarked *Contributors*: CoolKid1993

File:Craig-newmark.jpg *Source*: http://bibliocm.bibliolabs.com/mwAnon/index.php?title=File:Craig-newmark.jpg *License*: Attribution *Contributors*: Sierra Communications

Image:Craigslist01.jpg *Source*: http://bibliocm.bibliolabs.com/mwAnon/index.php?title=File:Craigslist01.jpg *License*: Creative Commons Attribution-Sharealike 2.5 *Contributors*: Calton, Jmabel, Mattbrundage, Rüdiger Wölk, Urban, 2 anonymous edits

File:Twttr sketch-Dorsey-2006.jpg *Source*: http://bibliocm.bibliolabs.com/mwAnon/index.php?title=File:Twttr_sketch-Dorsey-2006.jpg *License*: Creative Commons Attribution 2.0 *Contributors*: Jack Dorsey

Image:Twitter logo.svg *Source*: http://bibliocm.bibliolabs.com/mwAnon/index.php?title=File:Twitter_logo.svg *License*: unknown *Contributors*: Original uploader was GageSkidmore at en.wikipedia

File:Content of Tweets.svg *Source*: http://bibliocm.bibliolabs.com/mwAnon/index.php?title=File:Content_of_Tweets.svg *License*: Public Domain *Contributors*: User:Bryan.burgers, User:Quillaja

File:Twitter sf hq.jpg *Source*: http://bibliocm.bibliolabs.com/mwAnon/index.php?title=File:Twitter_sf_hq.jpg *License*: Creative Commons Attribution 2.0 *Contributors*: Olaf Koens

File:MarkZuckerberg.jpg *Source*: http://bibliocm.bibliolabs.com/mwAnon/index.php?title=File:MarkZuckerberg.jpg *License*: Creative Commons Attribution 2.5 *Contributors*: Elaine Chan and Priscilla Chan

File:Abc facebook debate saint anselm.JPG *Source*: http://bibliocm.bibliolabs.com/mwAnon/index.php?title=File:Abc_facebook_debate_saint_anselm.JPG *License*: Creative Commons Attribution-Sharealike 3.0 *Contributors*: User:Ericci8996

Image:Wiktionary-logo-en.svg *Source*: http://bibliocm.bibliolabs.com/mwAnon/index.php?title=File:Wiktionary-logo-en.svg *License*: Public Domain *Contributors*: User:Brion VIBBER

Image:commons-logo.svg *Source*: http://bibliocm.bibliolabs.com/mwAnon/index.php?title=File:Commons-logo.svg *License*: logo *Contributors*: User:3247, User:Grunt

File:Adwords logo.png *Source*: http://bibliocm.bibliolabs.com/mwAnon/index.php?title=File:Adwords_logo.png *License*: Trademarked *Contributors*: Google Inc.

File:901cherryave.jpg *Source*: http://bibliocm.bibliolabs.com/mwAnon/index.php?title=File:901cherryave.jpg *License*: GNU Free Documentation License *Contributors*: Alison, Infrogmation, JenVan, 1 anonymous edits

File:Flag of Argentina.svg *Source*: http://bibliocm.bibliolabs.com/mwAnon/index.php?title=File:Flag_of_Argentina.svg *License*: Public Domain *Contributors*: User:Dbenbenn

File:Flag of Australia.svg *Source*: http://bibliocm.bibliolabs.com/mwAnon/index.php?title=File:Flag_of_Australia.svg *License*: Public Domain *Contributors*: Ian Fieggen

File:Flag of Brazil.svg *Source*: http://bibliocm.bibliolabs.com/mwAnon/index.php?title=File:Flag_of_Brazil.svg *License*: Public Domain *Contributors*: Brazilian Government

File:Flag of Canada.svg *Source*: http://bibliocm.bibliolabs.com/mwAnon/index.php?title=File:Flag_of_Canada.svg *License*: Public Domain *Contributors*: User:E Pluribus Anthony, User:Mzajac

File:Flag of the Czech Republic.svg *Source*: http://bibliocm.bibliolabs.com/mwAnon/index.php?title=File:Flag_of_the_Czech_Republic.svg *License*: Public Domain *Contributors*: special commission (of code): SVG version by cs:-xfi-. Colors according to Appendix No. 3 of czech legal Act 3/1993. cs:Zirland.

File:Flag of France.svg *Source*: http://bibliocm.bibliolabs.com/mwAnon/index.php?title=File:Flag_of_France.svg *License*: Public Domain *Contributors*: User:SKopp, User:SKopp, User:SKopp, User:SKopp, User:SKopp, User:SKopp

File:Flag of Germany.svg *Source*: http://bibliocm.bibliolabs.com/mwAnon/index.php?title=File:Flag_of_Germany.svg *License*: Public Domain *Contributors*: User:Madden, User:Pumbaa80, User:SKopp

File:Flag of Hong Kong.svg *Source*: http://bibliocm.bibliolabs.com/mwAnon/index.php?title=File:Flag_of_Hong_Kong.svg *License*: Public Domain *Contributors*: Designed by

File:Flag of Israel.svg *Source*: http://bibliocm.bibliolabs.com/mwAnon/index.php?title=File:Flag_of_Israel.svg *License*: Public Domain *Contributors*: AnonMoos, Bastique, Bobika, Brown spite, Captain Zizi, Cerveaugenie, Drork, Etams, Fred J, Fry1989, Geagea, Himasaram, Homo lupus, Humus sapiens, Klemen Kocjancic, Kookaburra, Luispihormiguero, Madden, Neq00, NielsF, Nightstallion, Oren neu dag, Patstuart, PeeJay2K3, Pumbaa80, Ramiy, Reisio, SKopp, Sceptic, SomeDudeWithAUserName, Technion, Typhix, Valentinian, Yellow up, Zscout370, 31 anonymous edits

File:Flag of India.svg *Source*: http://bibliocm.bibliolabs.com/mwAnon/index.php?title=File:Flag_of_India.svg *License*: Public Domain *Contributors*: User:SKopp

File:Flag of Ireland.svg *Source*: http://bibliocm.bibliolabs.com/mwAnon/index.php?title=File:Flag_of_Ireland.svg *License*: Public Domain *Contributors*: User:SKopp

File:Flag of Italy.svg *Source*: http://bibliocm.bibliolabs.com/mwAnon/index.php?title=File:Flag_of_Italy.svg *License*: Public Domain *Contributors*: see below

File:Flag of Japan.svg *Source*: http://bibliocm.bibliolabs.com/mwAnon/index.php?title=File:Flag_of_Japan.svg *License*: Public Domain *Contributors*: Various

File:Flag of South Korea.svg *Source*: http://bibliocm.bibliolabs.com/mwAnon/index.php?title=File:Flag_of_South_Korea.svg *License*: Public Domain *Contributors*: Various

File:Flag of Mexico.svg *Source*: http://bibliocm.bibliolabs.com/mwAnon/index.php?title=File:Flag_of_Mexico.svg *License*: Public Domain *Contributors*: User:AlexCovarrubias

File:Flag of the Netherlands.svg *Source*: http://bibliocm.bibliolabs.com/mwAnon/index.php?title=File:Flag_of_the_Netherlands.svg *License*: Public Domain *Contributors*: User:Zscout370

File:Flag of New Zealand.svg *Source*: http://bibliocm.bibliolabs.com/mwAnon/index.php?title=File:Flag_of_New_Zealand.svg *License*: Public Domain *Contributors*: Adambro, Arria Belli, Avenue, Bawolff, Bjankuloski06en, ButterStick, Denelson83, Donk, Duduziq, EugeneZelenko, Fred J, Fry1989, Hugh Jass, Ibagli, Jusjih, Klemen Kocjancic, Mamndassan, Mattes, Nightstallion, O, Peeperman, Poromiami, Reisio, Rfc1394, Shizhao, Tabasco, Transparent Blue, Väsk, Xufanc, Zscout370, 35 anonymous edits

File:Flag of Poland.svg *Source*: http://bibliocm.bibliolabs.com/mwAnon/index.php?title=File:Flag_of_Poland.svg *License*: Public Domain *Contributors*: User:Mareklug, User:Wanted

File:Flag of Russia.svg *Source*: http://bibliocm.bibliolabs.com/mwAnon/index.php?title=File:Flag_of_Russia.svg *License*: Public Domain *Contributors*: Zscout370

CPSIA information can be obtained at www.ICGtesting.com
Printed in the USA
LVOW121936090812

293690LV00006BA/26/P